Walking the old ways of Radnorshire

Walking the old ways of Radnorshire

The history in the landscape explored through 26 circular walks

Andy & Karen Johnson

Logaston Press

LOGASTON PRESS
Little Logaston Woonton Almeley
Herefordshire HR3 6QH
www.logastonpress.co.uk

First published by Logaston Press September 2016

ISBN 978 1 910839 07 2

Typeset by Logaston Press
and printed and bound in Poland by www.lfbookservices.co.uk

Contents

Walk Location Map   *vi*

Introduction   *vii*

Walk 1 Llandrindod Wells   1
Walk 2 Cefnllys   11
Walk 3 Abbeycwmhir   19
Walk 4 Rhayader   25
Walk 5 St Harmon   31
Walk 6 Llananno, Tinboeth and Moelfre   37
Walk 7 Felindre and Castell y Blaidd   43
Walk 8 Knucklas   56
Walk 9 Knighton   55
Walk 10 Bleddfa   64
Walk 11 Pilleth   68
Walk 12 Cascob and Ednol   74
Walk 13 Norton and Offa's Dyke   80

Walk 14 Presteigne   90
Walk 15 New Radnor   102
Walk 16 Llanvihangel   112
Walk 17 The Pales   122
Walk 18 Llandegley   130
Walk 19 Hundred House   138
Walk 20 Glascwm   145
Walk 21 Rhulen   150
Walk 22 Painscastle and Llanbedr   158
Walk 23 Aberedw   169
Walk 24 Erwood   177
Walk 25 Llanstephan   183
Walk 26 Maesyronnen and Llowes   187

Index   195

Map of Radnorshire showing the locations of the walks

Key:

- A road
- B road
- Other tarmacked road
- Woodland
- Open Access Land (clear)
- Open Access Land (wooded)
- Stream or river
- Building or group of buildings
- Indication of slope from hill top
- Line of walk
- Other paths
- **1** Point on the map relating to same point in walk description
- Pub

The key above is to accompany the maps of the walk routes throughout the book.

Labels on map:

River Teme
7
Llanbadarn Fynydd
6
Llananno
Llanbister
St Harmon
5
3
Abbeycwmhir
4
RHAYADER
Llanbadarn Fawr
River Ithon
River Wye
2
1
LLANDRINDOD WELLS
18
Llandegley
17
Knucklas
8
River Lugg
9
KNIGHTON
Bleddfa
10
11
13
12
14
PRESTEIGNE
15
16
NEW RADNOR
River Edw
19
Hundred House
Glascwm
20
Rhulen
21
River Arrow
River Wye
22
Aberedw
23
24
Llandeilo Graban
25
Llanstephan
26
Llowes
Painscastle
Boughrood

Introduction

In devising these 26 walks we have tried to cover the whole of Radnorshire and a wide variety of historical sites – where they can be reached by footpath and with little use of main roads. Indeed, the nature of the terrain and the comparative paucity of roads means that several sites can *only* be reached by footpath, a very welcome feature when planning the walks we wished to include. Whilst Radnorshire's churches still have a very physical presence, only one castle (Castell Tinboeth) has any surviving masonry and that extremely minimal, whilst many of the tumuli can only be spotted when bracken cover has not yet reached its gung-ho phase, its standing stones are often below knee height and the one stone circle included involves much head scratching to be able to work it out. Offa's Dyke is prominent in places, but Cefn-y-Crug cross dyke could not be so described. Nevertheless, there is much to see and explore, including some 'oddities', such as a building blown up in the making of a film, a rare Roman fort where the street pattern can still be made out, and a mysterious grave on a ridgeway track.

The remains of the castle at Painscastle (seen just above the hedge) towards the end of walk 22

Each of Radnorshire's main towns down the centuries – New Radnor, Rhayader, Knighton, Presteigne and Llandrindod Wells – features in a walk, which also heads out of the settlement into the surrounding countryside. Other walks follow river valleys for at least part of their route, and many criss-cross hills and ridges, for here are old trackways and drovers roads, Bronze Age tumuli and standing stones, Iron Age hillforts and occasional baronial or princely castle. As a result many of the walks feature extensive views, as illustrated in the book. Because much of Radnorshire's border follows rivers, some walks stray into neighbouring counties so as to take in both sides of a valley.

Whilst the tracks across high ground and the country lanes maintained by Powys County Council provide good walking routes (the latter because they carry little traffic most of the time), it is the footpaths that link them that can be the most problematic in terms of easy walking. We ruled out some routes because of problems with stiles in poor repair or simply non existent, but have included some that might be difficult for the less sure of foot or malleable of body. We have mentioned these in the preamble to the relevant walk so that you are forewarned. We have walked several of the routes, or variations of them, many times over the years, so hopefully have chosen the 'best' option in terms of both ease of walking and providing pleasure and interest in what you can see en route.

Remember that paths do change. They can be (legally) diverted, new tracks may be created for ever larger farm

The view from Twyn y Garth on walk 24

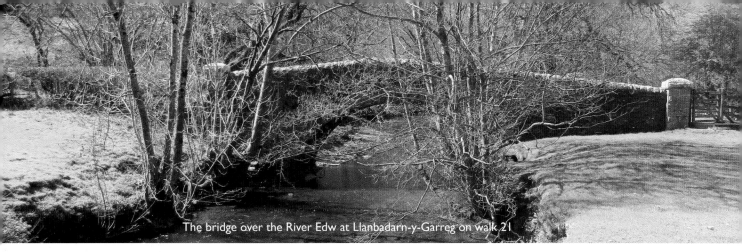

The bridge over the River Edw at Llanbadarn-y-Garreg on walk 21

machinery, trees or copses mentioned as landmarks may be felled or blown down. Likewise, pubs, cafés and museums open, close, re-open. Every time we've gone back to do a walk again, we've found that something is different. Bear in mind when out for a walk that you may need to adapt to conditions on the day.

We are very appreciative of the efforts of farmers to keep footpaths open, but there is only so much they can do. Vegetation will creep across paths as the spring turns to summer; winter rain may turn patches of ground into a sticky bog; gates get damaged by tractors or stock meaning they might become difficult to open and close. Always remember that you are legally allowed to find an alternative route round an obstruction if you find one on a public path. Of course, make sure that you close any gates you open, that if you're walking with a dog, you keep him

or her under control when you're walking among cattle, horses or sheep (llamas and alpacas might be spotted alongside some paths but not yet in fields they cross), and follow all the other aspects of the Countryside Code.

We've imagined that you'll probably be driving to the start of the walk. We haven't tried to provide information about driving routes to the walk locations but we've made some suggestions about finding particularly obscure places. Point 1 on each map marks where we've suggested you could park (often near a church or pub, sometimes in an unexpected rural car park or a lay-by of formal or other nature); making sure one parks safely sometimes requires a bit of effort on Radnorshire's little lanes.

The sketch maps for most of the walks are at a variable scale to each other; an indiction of the scale of each map can be derived from the total distance of the walk mentioned. It is advisable to take the relevant OS map with you as a back-up, even just to use to identify hills or features that you can see in the distance. We have marked the position of pubs and tea rooms where these feature on walks, or ones you may wish to visit at the start or end of a walk; we haven't included such symbols in the main towns, as they would tend to cover much of the map. In the case of some walks the only hope of sustenance en route will be to take it with you.

Each walk starts with a brief paragraph that gives its distance, an idea of the type of terrain underfoot and an indication as to how many stiles you are likely to face. A glance through the walk will tell you about the historic features that the walk includes. The paragraphs at the start of a few of the walks also indicate places en route which can be open to the public at certain times of the year or day, to give you a chance to plan in advance when to do the walk if you want to include such places. We have tried to give a reasonable depth of information about the places seen en route, but you may want to supplement it from other sources; church guides are available in many churches, for example.

All the photographs included with each walk have been taken on that walk (or on visits to places that can be included on the walk).

Andy & Karen Johnson
July 2016

A path between Maesyronnen and Llowes on walk 26

Walk 1
Llandrindod Wells

7 miles mostly on well-formed paths and pavements, some roads and across fields to Castell Collen and by the Ithon. There are no stiles. Includes a landscaped lake and park, features of Llandrindod's townscape, the springs and spa in Rock Park and the remains of Castell Collen Roman fort. There are tea rooms near the start and end of the walk, and en route in Rock Park.

Park in the little car park by the lake, or on Princes Avenue, the road that serves this car park and the nearby tearooms in the old boat house.

❶ Start by walking along the road round the lake, keeping the lake to your right. The dragon fountain, The Fabulous Water Beast, was created by Richard Taylor, a coppersmith sculptor. Very much a community project, over 1,000 people inscribed their initials or wrote a message on the beast's scales.

❷ Take the second footpath off to the left (there is a bench on a small green on the other side of the road at this point). This path soon starts to fairly steeply ascend the wooded slope, in part by some steps. Near the top the path forks and you keep to the right. Almost immediately

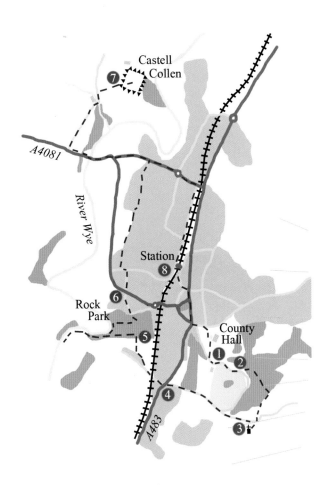

you cross another path and leave the woodland through a small wooden gate, and then turn right. Follow this path along and it will lead you up onto a small patch of meadow with views to the Church of the Holy Trinity. Keep to the path and leave the meadow through a wooden gate. Cross the road to visit the church and churchyard.

CHURCH OF THE HOLY TRINITY

The church lies to the south-east of the modern settlement of Llandrindod Wells, on ground rising quite steeply to what was common land. The earthworks on the opposite side of the road to the north possibly mark the sites of former houses. The present church dates from 1894, replacing what was probably a 13th- or 14th-century building. A sheila-na-gig, a carving of a woman opening her vulva, from the earlier church is now in the town's museum. Some have claimed that such carvings are a folkloric remembrance of pagan fertility cults, but as this one was displayed on a church, it was more likely a warning of the perils of the flesh. In 1911 the church was extended to the west with the addition of another 'bay' and a new vestry. In 1920, the first archbishop of Wales was elected here.

3 Leave the churchyard and turn left down Grosvenor Road, following it all the way down to a T-junction with the A483. En route you'll pass by the lake again and later a line of oaks on your right, marked by a plaque which records they were grown from acorns taken from Windsor Great Park to mark the coronation of George VI in 1937.

4 Cross the A483 and take the left-hand road of the two roads opposite (to the left of the red brick building with an iron and glass veranda along its front). This leads under a railway bridge. After a further 100 yards and just before you reach a house, take the path off to the right. This soon passes alongside what was once a school playing field, of which part has become a green and community orchard. The path will turn to the right, and on the next stretch you will pass between the sites of two practice Roman camps, though it is difficult to discern any traces of them. These were built in miniature here (and in what are now fields behind you) by the soldiers based at Castle Collen (see below) to practise the techniques of constructing marching camps, erected to provide temporary protection when the Roman army was on the move.

5 Shortly after these sites you enter the woods of Rock Park. Keep ahead to descend the slope by steps or flat path to the Spa Buildings, now home to a coffee house and tea room, as well as a complementary medicine treatment centre. Turn half left and back up the slope towards some bungalows, then bear right to pass to the left of the Bowling Club. On your left you will reach a large oak, under which Baptists are said to have held their meetings before they were allowed to build a chapel.

Carry on along the track, keeping to the left. You can keep going down this track and so down to a kissing gate into the field at the bottom and then walk along by the river till the path ends at the end of the field (there used to be stepping stones across the river), but you have to return by the same way. On the way to and from the kissing gate you pass Lovers' Leap, said to be where a couple, forbidden to marry, threw themselves into the river in despair.

The circular walk continues by turning down the steps on the right as you descend towards the kissing gate, and taking the path above the river, now on your left. When you come to a junction of paths, turn right and you'll soon reach the end of

SPA

The iron, sulphur and saline waters of Llandrindod were known to the Romans, who are said to have called the springs Balinae Silures. The first recorded use of the sulphurous waters at Llandrindod was in 1696 by members of one of the Herefordshire Vaughan families, but the waters seem to have been largely neglected till 'rediscovered' in 1736 by Mrs Jenkins, tenant of Bach y Craig farm on what was then a bleak common but where the county hall, lake and park now stand. Other springs were soon brought into play, including a chalybeate (rich in iron), in what is now Rock Park (originally Cwm-y-gof, or Blacksmith's Dingle). Soon articles were appearing in *The Gentleman's Magazine* and other publications talking of various 'cures', and a rash of speculative building followed. In 1748 a Mr Grosvenor from Shrewsbury converted Llandrindod Hall, a neglected farmhouse near the parish church, into a hotel, created a racecourse, made a cockpit and bowling green, installed billiard tables, created a large ballroom and fitted up a theatre. However, the hotel soon had a reputation for gambling and clandestine love affairs and its owner, apparently in a fit of contrition, had it demolished, though other reports tell of it being destroyed by a fire. For a while the town became a dull resort for the physically infirm. Nevertheless, by the early 1800s the spa had a modest following. In 1809 names of 'fashionable arrivals' were reported in the Hereford papers, but the spa really began to blossom with the coming of railways in the 1850s and '60s when a plethora of hotels and guest houses were opened. By the end of the 1800s it was estimated that some 90,000 people a year were visiting the spa, the town then boasting two assembly rooms, a pavilion, a pump room, over a dozen hotels and many guest houses.

By the 1820s, Bach y Craig farm had become a large boarding house known as The Pump House, and was subsequently developed into a hotel offering two tariffs aimed at different markets; the two sections of the hotel were soon known as The House of Lords and The House of Commons. In the 1860s, the Trefonen Estate, of which Bach y Craig farm was but part, was inherited by Edward Middleton Evans who had plans drawn up for a major hotel, a bath house offering various treatments, and pleasure grounds, including a lake. In 1888 the new Pump House Hotel opened and a further wing comprising 150 rooms was added in 1900. The pleasure grounds covered some 100 acres and apart from the lake, included tennis courts, croquet lawns and promenades. During the 'season' from May to mid September, queues would form to access the pump rooms at the hotel and those in Rock Park, and would be entertained by orchestras. With the decline in popularity of spas in the 1900s the hotel went through several different uses (a military hospital, a teacher training college and a residential school for deaf children) before becoming the headquarters for the newly formed Powys County Council in 1974. The building was subsequently declared structurally unsound and was replaced in 1991 by the present County Hall, which stands slightly to the east of its predecessor.

the bowling greens, Turn left at this point, following the path round the edge of the greens, passing a carved 'Llandoddie' en route. There are several Llandoddies around the town, carvings based on the mythical water creatures of Llandrindod Wells created by local author and artist David Bellamy, writing under the pseudonym Griswallt ap Llechitwyt.

After the path has turned to the right to follow the edge of the greens, take the first path off to the left, soon reaching a hexagonal wooden structure marking the site of one of the spa's saline wells. The path continues to another structure, this time marking a sulphur well. Keep on the path and it will lead you to the roadway round the front

of the spa building. Cross this to a wooden bridge across the Arlais brook. To the right of the bridge, steps lead down to the Eye Well. Cross the bridge and turn right to reach a cobbled area with carved wooden seats (known as the Four Kings and designed by a local student) and the chalybeate spring. The water is high in salts and iron and is said to cure tiredness, amongst other things.

Return to the bridge and cross over the path, to keep to the right-hand bank of the Arlais brook. This will lead you to the road that serves the spa, on which you turn right and so walk up to a T-junction. Turn left here and follow the road which will bend to the right and meet another.

6 Cross this and walk ahead down Victoria Road. When you reach the end of the road and face a school, cross the road, turn left and walk down some tens of yards till you reach a tarmacked footpath off to the right. Take this and walk between the school buildings and a sports pitch, jinking right and left further on to meet another road. Cross this onto Holcombe Avenue, and turn right at its end to walk up to a main road. Turn left on this and follow it down to the junction with the A4081. Turn right on this and follow the path, often separated from the A road by a hedge, over the Ithon to take the next road right. Follow this and pass by a farm on your left. Then look for a gate at right angles to the road on your right. Through this, follow the hedge on your right: a permissive path will take you to a gate into the fields where lies Castell Collen.

CASTELL COLLEN

The Roman strategy in Wales was based on a quadrilateral of four great military stations: Caerleon (Isca), Chester (Deva), Caernarvon (Segontium) and Carmarthen (Maridunum). The corners of this quadrilateral were linked by roads, and other roads crossed its interior, usually running along river valleys. Auxiliary forts were placed along these roads at intervals of a day's march, and in mid Wales the three key forts were the Gaer near Brecon, Caersws in Montgomeryshire and Castell Collen. The latter was built on a spur jutting into the Ithon, its elevated position helping to keep the fort well drained.

In 1804 the site was visited by Sir Richard Colt Hoare and Richard Fenton, who saw the foundations of several stone buildings, together with pieces of brick and fragments of pottery. Cartloads of dressed stone had already been taken from the site to build farmhouses, and more went during the 1800s. The first excavations were not carried out until 1911-13, and were aimed at finding and tracing the walls within the Roman fort. The excavators unearthed inscribed stones and pottery and then began to excavate the headquarters building at the centre of the main street and, to the south of the main street, the commandant's house, which comprised three ranges of rooms around a courtyard. The granary to the north of the main street was also found, and the excavations in general suggested that the troops were essentially fed a vegetarian diet. More major excavations were undertaken between 1954 and 1957 by Leslie Alcock. Trenches were dug

across the ramparts and all the gates were examined, while a series of minor excavations were carried out within the encompassing walls. Two extra-mural bath houses were also investigated.

As a result of these excavations a rough history of the site has been proposed. An original fort of a turf bank some 25 feet wide and 5 feet high fronted by a palisade and a water-filled ditch seems to have been built by Julius Frontinus during his campaign of AD75-78 against the Silures. In the middle of the 2nd century AD the defences were revetted in stone, the height of the banks behind raised (and braced at the rear with timber stakes) and stone gateways built. These gateways had projecting semi-circular facades, at a time when such a design was a novelty. The original ditch had silted up, so a wider second ditch was dug a little further out and again water-filled. An inscribed stone found in one of the bath houses suggests that this work was carried out by the 2nd Augustan Legion.

In the early part of the 3rd century the fort was reduced in size by about one fifth, the western defences levelled and a new west gate of irregular rectangular form constructed with a simple passageway flanked by two guard chambers. Now square in shape and with quarters for some 400 to 500 men, it had half the accommodation of the original fort. The reduction came at a time when troops were needed to counter threats in other parts of the Empire. In the late 3rd or early 4th century, during the time of Emperors Carausius and Constantius Chlorus when a reorganisation of the defences in Britain was undertaken, the walls and gates were renovated and ditches recut.

It would appear that the fort might have been abandoned at periods between its rebuilding phases, as some of walls have been shown to have been rebuilt from their foundations as the result of a substantial collapse, an unlikely event if an active garrison was continually maintaining its defences. A civil settlement appears to have existed to the south-east of the fort.

7 Having had a look around, return to the bridge on the A4081 across the Ithon, and turn left on the first bend (so continuing to retrace your steps). However, this time keep on ahead, cross the roundabout and immediately before the railway line take the road off to the right. Follow this along, and keep ahead when it meets a more major road, to pass Tescos on your right.

8 When you reach a footbridge across the railway line on your left, cross this, observing the signal box over to the right, and the glazed veranda roof on the far platform on the left. The signal box stood at a level crossing in the town before it became redundant in 1986 due to changes in technology, and it was moved to its present position a few years later. It is occasionally open to the public. The veranda roof used to adorn the front of the Pump House Hotel.

Turn right up Station Crescent. You may wish to turn right into Middleton Street to see the variety of independent shops, but the walk continues ahead to the A483/ Temple Street, on which you turn right. On the left, you pass the town museum and the Metropole Hotel and at the road junction then reached (Fiveways), you turn left into Spa Road East. Walk up this, then take the right turn signposted for County Hall. When you reach the lake in front of County Hall, follow the road round to the right and you'll soon see what was originally the boiler house of the Pump House Hotel (for which see the information on the Spa on page 5).

Take the path off to the right opposite the ex-boiler house, bearing left and then immediately right when you meet another path, to emerge onto grass alongside the road on which you parked or approached the car park by the lake. Before returning to your car, or trying the tea rooms, turn left on the grass and you'll quickly come to the ruins of Capel Maelog.

CAPEL MAELOG

This is the remains of a 12th- or 13th-century chapel, moved to this location. In the late 1980s excavation in what is now an eastern suburb of Llandrindod Wells revealed the remains of an early church. Known as Llandemaylon and Llanvayloir in 1291, the church seems to have fallen into disuse and was not mentioned in a survey of churches in 1533. The excavations revealed, due to finding scatters of flints, that the site had been used in prehistoric times. It was then used for secular purposes in the late Roman and post-Roman periods, followed by agricultural use before being used for a small cemetery immediately preceding the building of the church, the site then surrounded by low earthen banks.

The first church comprised a nave about 15 feet wide and 21 feet long and a chancel of about half those dimensions, and was built of dry-stone walling with an earth floor. Some time later the chancel and west wall of the nave were replaced with curved apses, so creating one space, curved on both its eastern and western ends. It's probable that brick and tile from the Roman fort at Castell Collen was used to create the window openings and other parts of the building. Some 350 burials were found within and around the church, notably to its east. The church was rebuilt in the 12th or 13th century, and it is the footprint of this church that now stands near the lake, having been moved from its original location to preserve it.

Walk 2
Cefnllys

4.5 miles, on a mixture of footpaths, quiet roads and tracks. There is a bit of a climb up to the site of Cefnllys Castle, but worth the views and the interest of the site itself, otherwise the walk is in gently rolling country. There are some stiles. The Ithon is crossed on two footbridges.

In Penybont take the A44 west. Immediately after you have crossed the bridge over the Ithon, take the minor road to the left. Take the first turning to the right, signposted Llanbadarn Fawr (about a mile after the bridge) and when you come to a no through road sign which stands at the beginning of a metalled lane leading straight ahead (the road you're on bends to the right at this point), find a place to park.

❶ Walk on down the no through road, which passes a new house and older buildings and then another new house on the right, before heading towards another older farm. Shortly before you reach this second farm, at a point where there's a farm shed on the left and the entrance to a motocross track on the right, cross the stile on

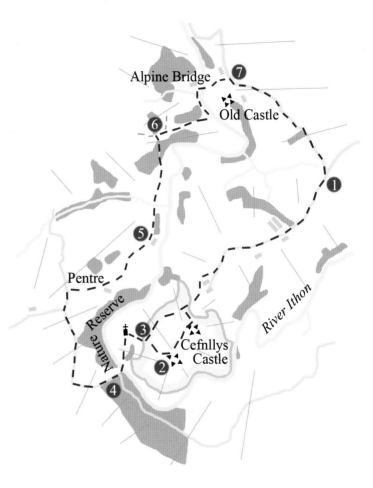

Alpine Bridge
Old Castle
Pentre
Nature Reserve
Cefnllys Castle
River Ithon

CEFNLLYS CASTLE

Cefnllys means hilltop court and it is thought that Elystan Glodrydd built some form of hall or fortification here in the 10th century, on what is believed to be the site of an Iron Age hillfort. Elystan Glodrydd was the founder of the fifth royal line in Wales (the three principal lines being North Wales or Gwynedd, South Wales or Deheubarth, and Powys), and is recorded as being King of Rhwng Gwy a Hafren, 'Between Wye and Severn'. Elystan is a Welsh rendering of Athelstan, a name he is thought to have been given as a result of his father being a godson of King Athelstan of England (927-939), who was recognised by the Welsh as High King of Britain.

The present remains are of two castles. The earliest, built between 1240 and 1246 by the Mortimers, is at the northern end (that first reached when you ascend the hill) where, on an elliptical 'motte', a rectangular keep was built with an approach ramp on its south-western side. However, it is possible that the motte is itself made of the partially collapsed tower. A bailey extends to the north with the remains of another collapsed tower at the north-west point, and a triangular bailey lies to the south-west. Around this, various tumps indicate other collapsed towers. Outside the bailey on the western side was a long thin ward, against the outside wall of which a platform indicates there was once a hall-like building.

This castle had not been long built when it was taken by Llywelyn ap Gruffudd in 1262, apparently by 'treachery', and the buildings set on fire. A relieving force under Roger (II) Mortimer and Humphrey de Bohun were then besieged in the broken walls by Llywelyn, who eventually allowed the force to make an ignominious retreat. This phase of Anglo-Welsh hostilities was ended by the Treaty of Montgomery, signed in 1267, one clause of which specifically allowed Mortimer to repair Cefnllys whilst discussion of the lawful right to ownership of Maelienydd, a Welsh cantref that now forms the north-eastern part of Radnorshire, was put on hold.

Mortimer quickly exploited the clause, and rather than just repair the existing castle, which work he commenced in 1268, he then started building a second, stronger tower to its south between 1272 and 1274. This was divided from the rest of the site by a rock-cut ditch, still clearly visible. Between this and the new tower was a wall and a gatehouse, whilst on the southern side of the tower was a small ward, seemingly lightly defended. The 'new' structure at Cefnllys was the cause of a complaint by Llywelyn in 1273/4 as being outside the terms of the Treaty, but Henry III was more than happy to see the Mortimer stronghold flourish, and by 1277 Llywelyn was no longer in a position to seek redress. In any event, the new fortifications failed to prevent the castle being captured in 1294.

In 1406 it was garrisoned with 12 spearmen and 30 archers against Owain Glyndwr, whose forces ravaged the local lands, but it is unclear if they took the castle, for it remained inhabited in the following years (which it might not have been if destroyed in the wars) and between 1432 and 1459 once again had a constable. The poet Lewys Glyn Cothi wrote four poems about the castle at this time, praising the constable's hospitality. The poems also mention a new timber-framed hall and an octagonal tower. By the time John Leland visited the site in 1539 or '40, all had become a ruin.

The Mortimers intended to form a borough here and by 1304 it comprised 25 families, a mill on the river and presumably a bridge as pontage was being charged. It seems to have declined from that point, with 20 families recorded in 1332 and just 10 in 1382. Nevertheless, it was still one of the five Radnorshire boroughs that returned a joint Member of Parliament under the 1536 Act of Union. The borough was probably centred on the church, around which a few house platforms can be seen, notably to the church's north and east.

your right and follow the grassy track. This will take you past the farmhouse on your left. At the gateway beyond the farm, bear right downhill. Here you can see the river on your right across the fields. The site of Cefnllys Castle soon towers above you on the left. You can either carry on along the track to a gate (see ❸ below) or, to see the castle site, take the grassy path up the steep bank on the left, and at the top, follow the ridge along; the high point of the castle is straight ahead, and if you're feeling energetic, you could climb to the top – the reward is a fabulous view.

CHURCH OF ST MICHAEL

Formerly the centre of a borough sited below the castle, the church now stands isolated amongst fields harbouring the remains of trackways and house foundations. The church is believed to date to the 13th century, though probably only some of the lower courses of the walls now remain from this build. However, the circular nature of the churchyard and the ancient yews suggests a much earlier Christian origin. Inside the church, the screen dates to the 15th century, and the font, piscina and aumbry all pre-date the Reformation. Rebuilding of at least parts of the walls seems to have occurred during the 16th and 17th centuries, and in the latter century some wood from the pews was used to make the pulpit. In 1893 the rector of Llandrindod Wells had the roof of the church removed to try to encourage the parishioners to head into town to attend his new church – photos inside the church show it in this condition. His attempt failed, however, for in 1895 the tops of the walls were rebuilt, together with most the tower, a new hammerbeam and arch-braced roof was constructed and the screen of c.1500 was restored, though it still bears the scars of having being open to the elements.

2 To then reach the church, take the steep path down the hillside from below the castle's high point, with the church slightly to your right. When you're about three-quarters of the way down the hillside, take the path off to the right towards the church. This will lead you down to a field gate above the church, at a point where it also meets the track on which you had been walking before you clambered up to the castle.

3 Go through the gate and head towards the church, passing through a second gate to enter the churchyard.

On leaving the church, almost opposite the porch you'll see a gate into the surrounding pasture. Go through the gate and walk through the pasture down to the river, aiming for a point below the right-hand edge of the steep conifer-clad hillside, and cross the river by a footbridge. Immediately over the bridge on the right is a nature reserve in the care of the Radnorshire Wildlife Trust which you may want to visit before continuing the walk.

BAILEY EINON NATURE RESERVE
This is an 11-acre reserve consisting largely of ancient semi-natural woodland, with alder and ash predominating in the wetter areas, and oak and hazel in the drier. An information board at the entrance to the reserve indicates what wildlife might be seen.

4 From the bridge, bear right and uphill on the tarmacked lane. This will take you round to the right, and at the first junction on the crest of the rise you keep straight ahead. However, at the next junction, in a dip just in front of a bungalow, turn right. This track will lead you to the farmyard of the Pentre. Just before the yard there's a footpath sign directing you to the left of all the buildings. Follow this path round some barns and go through a gate at their far end; turn left on a track and leave the farmyard past the sheep handling equipment on the left. On the right is Pentre mound which is a probable castle motte, but no excavation has taken place to try to discover its provenance.

The track enters a field and the footpath now follows the field boundary on your right, passing an overgrown gateway, then passing through a gateway into the next field. Again follow the field boundary on your right. This will lead downhill to a gateway in the corner of the field, through which you pass and turn half right and walk down the hillside, aiming just to the left of the house in the valley bottom. As you near this you will see a stile in the hedge-line ahead.

5 Cross this stile and go over the track to the one on the far side. The path now shadows the edge of some woodland on your right and crosses a stile into the next field. Cross this field to its far right-hand corner where you cross another stile. From here the path heads towards the woodland ahead of you, aiming just to the left of a large oak which stands right in the hedge that borders the wood. As you near the oak, you need to keep to the right of a small area of marshy ground with rushes to reach the stile into the wood. Cross this stile, turn left and then immediately right and follow the path slanting up through the woodland, which follows a bank to its right. At the top of the wood, near a large boulder, go through a gate into the field beyond and straight up the hillside to the right of a line of trees.

6 At the top you'll meet a path; turn right along it, passing round a grove of oaks. You'll shortly come to a choice of paths; keep straight on down the middle of a narrow field, go through a gate and bear slightly left down through the next field. Keep heading downhill till you reach the river, and go through the gate on your left to walk along the river bank (the river being to your

CEFNLLYS OLD CASTLE
Whilst this is certainly the site of a castle motte now standing about 5m high which would have been topped by a wooden tower and which was almost certainly built by the Mortimers before they built the castles on the ridge seen at the start of the walk, opinions differ as to which Mortimer built it and when. One line of thought it that was built by Roger (I) Mortimer not long after the Mortimers became established at Wigmore in Herefordshire and made advances into central Wales. Another line of thought is that this was the castle called Dineithon built by Roger's son Ralph Mortimer in the 1090s.

right) and then uphill to a corner of a field where you'll find a gate onto a track. Go through this and turn right. Just ahead you'll see a small gate on the right; go through this and follow the path down to the Alpine Bridge, where the River Ithon rushes through a gorge. Once over the bridge, keep to the right of two large oaks, then follow the top of a bank on your left. (As you cross this field keep an eye out for the motte of Cefnllys old castle atop the slope to your right.) When the bank fades away, keep ahead to cross the field, on the far side turning right to follow the line of trees. Just after the line of trees meets a hedge you'll reach a stile, which you cross and follow a short path down to a road.

❼ Turn right on the road, bearing left at the split you almost immediately reach, and this will bring you back to where you parked.

Walk 3
Abbeycwmhir

4.75 miles on a mixture of footpaths, tracks and quiet roads. The ascents of the two hillsides are fairly gentle, but the descent on a track through forestry near the end of the walk is steep and can be muddy. There are just three stiles, but one possibly awkward gateway (depending upon whether it has been repaired or not). You may wish to check the opening hours of the Happy Union pub, and also of Abbeycwmhir Hall, should you wish to visit it (see page 22).

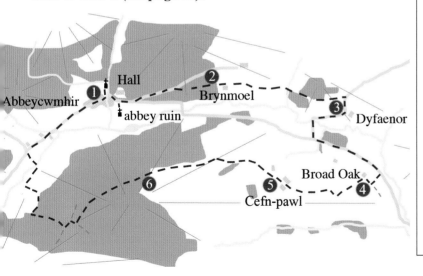

Park near the church in Abbeycwmhir.

CHURCH OF ST MARY, ABBEYCWMHIR

The church at Abbeycwmhir, once possibly dedicated to St Bridget but now to St Mary, was built in 1865-66, replacing an earlier church erected in 1680 by Richard Fowler (who then owned the Abbeycwmhir estate) that lay slightly to the south. It is believed that the monks of Abbeycwmhir may have had a fish pond near the site, and it's probable that the abbey ruins might have provided much of the stone for the church. An unusual aspect of the church's plan is the tower over the porch. Over the doorway is a carving of the Ascension, copied from a tympanum that was once at the abbey. The church contains a coffin lid of Abbot Mabli dated *c.*1200.

19

❶ With your back to the church, turn left on the road and just round the bend, go through the gate on the right to see the ruins of Cwmhir Abbey.

CWMHIR ABBEY

The Cistercian abbey was founded in 1143, but only appears to have been fully operational by 1176, under the patronage of Cadwallon ap Madog. At some point thereafter a massive programme of rebuilding began, with a nave measuring 242 feet long and 80 wide; that at Westminster Abbey is only 235 feet long. But when was it rebuilt and by whom?

Many consider the man responsible to be Llywelyn ab Iorwerth (Fawr) who wished to extend his control more firmly in central Wales, and Maelienydd in particular. Whilst Llywelyn had seized the area during the troubled end of the reign of King John in 1216, by the mid 1220s his hold on the region had become precarious: the abbey had to pay Henry III to secure the king's goodwill and the Mortimers were asked to return some territory in the area to Llywelyn as he and Henry were in discussion about a more permanent peace treaty. Warfare was never far away, however. In 1228 Henry III led an abortive campaign into Maelienydd, and warfare broke out again in 1231 and 1233. The truce of Myddle (in Shropshire) in 1234 then left matters relatively peaceful till Llywelyn's death in 1240. During the warfare in 1231 a monk of Cwmhir is reputed to have tricked the English into an ambush resulting in heavy casualties, but as a result an abbey grange was burned and the abbey was plundered. The abbot also had to pay 300 marks to save the abbey's buildings, a sum which suggests they were of some extent. Thus if the building was encouraged and funded by Llywelyn, then construction is likely to have taken place in the 1220s. But the Grinshill stone used for some of the walling will have come from Shropshire, and lime for the mortar most likely from near Kington, though it could have come from elsewhere, areas not under Llywelyn's control. So could someone else have been responsible?

At the dissolution some of the stiff leaf sculpture with which the abbey was decorated as part of this rebuilding, was moved to Llanidloes Church. The carving mirrors the progress in style in England between the late 12th century and its full development in the first decade of the 1200s. As the Mortimers had regained Maelienydd in 1195 (till they lost it again in 1216), it would seem likely that they were responsible for the rebuilding in the first decade of the 13th century.

Whoever was responsible, the abbey certainly grew in importance when Llywelyn ap Gruffudd was buried here in 1282. Despite this, it was partially destroyed by Owain Glyndwr in 1402 as it was believed the monks this time were passing information on the Welsh rising to the English. It probably never recovered as it was valued at very little at the time of its dissolution. The Fowler family acquired the ruins and lands in about 1562 and built a house. Royalists who fortified the ruins in 1644 surrendered to Parliamentarian forces after being battered by cannon fire which also appears to have destroyed the Fowlers' house.

ABBEYCWMHIR HALL

The house was built by Thomas Wilson, a London businessman who acquired the estate in 1822. In 1837 the estate was bought by Francis Philips of Manchester, who had made his fortune in the textile business. It passed to Francis' second son, George, who remodelled the house in the late 1860s. George was selected to stand in the Conservative interest in the Radnor Boroughs seat at a by-election in 1869, but was decisively defeated by the Liberals. By 1873 the estate extended to 6,236 acres. Its current owners, the Humpherstons, have recently completed a 10-year period of further restoration and now offer tours of the 52-room, grade II house and associated 12 acres of grounds, which include walled gardens, lawns, courtyards, a lake and a waterfall. To book a tour email info@abbeycwmhir.com or phone 01597 851727. Visitors are asked to pre-book whenever possible, otherwise you might find the hall closed for the day.

Return to the road and turn right, passing the Hall on your left. Immediately past its entrance drive, fork left up the tarmacked lane. Presently a track joins this from the left, and then leaves it to the right – you want to take this right fork, and for a while you will be walking Glyndwr's Way.

2 When the track reaches the entrance to the red brick house Brynmoel, Glyndwr's Way goes through the gate on the left and then follows the boundary fence on your right. Once past Brynmoel, Glyndwr's Way turns half right and drops down to a small gate adjacent to a field gate in the fenceline. Go through this, and then turn left to follow the fence (and old sunken way) on your left through two fields, joining a gravelled track in the second of these. Just before this track bends to the right, follow the fence on your left round the grounds of a small cottage well buried in the trees.

You will quickly reach a small gate that leads to a path down to a footbridge across a stream, and then a path up the far bank. Near the top of the bank you cross a stile on the left and go up a shaley path to find yourself in (appropriately) a small shale quarry. Cross the track that serves this and continue on the path through the woodland until it meets a stile. Cross this stile and cross the field keeping to your contour (i.e. maintaining your height above sea level!) to a stile on the far side. Cross this and drop down onto a lane. Turn right on the lane and soon you'll pass the yellow painted Dyfaenor.

DYFAENOR

This was originally a hunting lodge set within a great park said to be 7 miles in circumference and stocked with upwards of 200 deer. It was remodelled in 1670 by Richard Fowler, after his main house had been destroyed during the Civil Wars, with a central staircase with a room to each side on each floor. The basement comprised the servants' hall and kitchen, the ground floor the dining parlour and hall, the first floor two bedrooms with a loft floor above.

3 Continue on the road to a T-junction where you turn left. You almost immediately pass one gravelled track off to the right, but it is the second such track you want to take, reached after about a third of a mile and with a red Royal Mail post box at the entrance. Walk up the track and at the T-junction soon reached, turn right and walk along to the red brick Broad Oak.

4 Go through their entrance gateway, and then take the small gate off to the left and follow the field boundary on your left uphill. When this boundary turns to the left, keep on straight ahead up and across the field, heading for a point some halfway along the far field boundary. Once you reach this, turn right and walk along it to a gate in the corner of the field. Go through this and walk along the track on its far side which will lead to another gate close to the farm buildings of Cefn-pawl.

pond and shadow the field boundary on your right to a small gate into the recently felled and replanted woodland ahead. Along this stretch you get good views of the village.

6 Through the gate you join a track that initially rises slightly uphill, then drops downhill to meet another track. Turn right on this and in a few yards you'll come to another junction of tracks. Turn left here, then look for and take a small path off to the right reached in about 30 yards. This leads downhill, passing just to the left of a stand of tall trees. When it meets a larger track, turn right and this will plunge you downhill through the stand of tall trees. At the bottom of the plantation the track swings right, and then left to reach a gate into a field. Go through the gate and follow the hedge on your right, the track swinging right and then left to reach a junction of roads. Turn right on the road to return to Abbeycwmhir.

5 Follow the track between the red brick farm buildings, passing the empty (in 2016) farmhouse on your right and through a gateway into the next field. Keep left where the track splits after just a few yards, following the fenceline on the left. Go through a gateway you reach across the track shortly after passing a large oak, and then turn left (away from the track) and follow the fenceline uphill on your left. After about 100 yards, where the fence bears slightly to the left, turn slightly right and continue on across the field to join a track which leads to a gate into the field beyond. Go through this gate and follow the track which leads to a man-made pond. Stay to the left of this

---

THE HAPPY UNION

This brick and stone grade II listed building with cast iron windows is one of the oldest in the village, and may once have been a drovers' inn. The name is said to refer to the Union between England and Wales in 1536. On this basis, the colourful inn sign has been read as a happy Welshman (his hat is decorated with a leek) with a  pint of ale in one hand and a plate of bread and cheese in the other, riding a goat representing an Englishman.

Walk 4
Rhayader

6 miles on a mixture of tracks, roads and footpaths. The walk explores the older part of Rhayader and the castle site, then takes you into gentle hills to the west of the town before returning through Llansantffraed Cwmdeuddwr. There are several inns and tea rooms in the town.

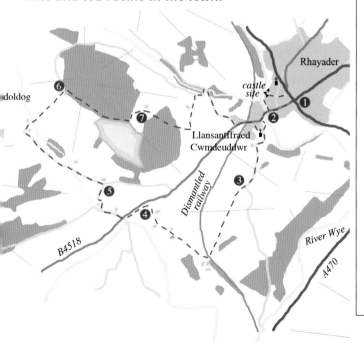

Park in Rhayader.

1 From the clock tower, head along North Street (the A470 heading towards Llangurig) and take Cross Lane, the first road off to the left, just before the cattle market. At the crossroads, turn right to visit St Clement's Church.

CHURCH OF ST CLEMENT, RHAYADER

Now dedicated to St Clement, the church was traditionally dedicated to the 6th-century St Cynllo, whose great-grandfather was the brother of Helen, the mother of Constantine the Great. St Cynllo is believed to have had a cell at Llanbister. Despite the Normans' rededication of the church, a poem by Lewis Glyn Cothi in 1460 tells of his intent to visit Rhayader on 17 July to celebrate St Cynllo's day.

The church seems to have been rebuilt several times. One predecessor of the present building fell down about 1772, itself a replacement of an earlier medieval church that might have stood closer to the castle as the current church stands outside the line of the putative town defences. The church built in 1772 was described as 'a plain but neat edifice [in which] a timber partition separates the chancel from the nave .... The old church was much more spacious than the present one, containing an aisle on each side of the nave and chancel.' The tower of the new church was erected in 1783 and, in digging the foundations, a large number of skeletons were discovered about a foot below the ground surface (for which see under the entry for Rhayader Castle).

The present church was built by S.W. Williams of Rhayader between 1887 and 1897 in the Early English style. The north aisle appears to have been a late addition in 1897. The font survives from the medieval church.

RHAYADER

Rhayader was initially called Rayadyr Gwy, 'Waterfall on the Wye', the water-fall (now rapids since the river bed was altered when the new bridge was built in 1780, replacing one of timber built slightly further up the river) being just below the bridge on the road that joins the two settlements of Llansantffraid Cwmdeuddwr and Rhayader. Llansantffraid Cwmdeuddwr was the earlier settlement, built where the ground alongside the Wye is relatively flat and broad. The name Rayadyr Gwy is first recorded in 1177, Rhayader in 1295. A town is first mentioned in 1304 and by 1360 rents were being collected from burgages. No charter has been found, so it was a borough 'by prescription', formed as a result of long-standing unchallenged custom, though markets and a fair had been granted by charter in the 13th century. The market lay at the junction of the two main streets, one that ran east/west and the other north/south. Earthwork defences have been identified in places surrounding the town, and the creation of such defences can be inferred from various documents. The town suffered at the hands of Glyndwr, but subsequently became a local market centre and for a brief while was the home of the county court until it transferred to Presteigne. The town was home to a small woollen industry in the 18th century, with three mills still operating early in the 19th century.

The earliest houses were built near the planned right-angled junction of the two main roads 200m east of the castle, though much of the street pattern here represents the usual medieval 'huddle' of buildings.

Amongst the oldest buildings in the town are the Royal Oak and the 17th-century stone house to its rear; what was the Cwmdeuddwr Arms (now a bike shop) also of the 17th century; and the Old Swan, which was an inn, then a Tourist Information Centre and is now tea rooms, is a timber-framed building dating to 1683. Opposite, the corner shop on the south side of East Street also has early to mid 17th-century origins. A town hall built in 1762 was demolished in 1922.

Return to the crossroads and turn right down Castle Road
to soon reach the site of Rhayader Castle on the left.

RHAYADER CASTLE

Rhayader is the site of two castles, one Welsh, one Norman-English, on the
west and east banks of the Wye respectively. The Welsh built their castle
first, on a site near the church in Cwmdeuddwr, that part of the town on
the west bank. It was founded in 1177 by, according to Gerald of Wales,
Rhys ap Gruffudd of Deheubarth and was certainly complete by 1184 when
Rhys signed a charter granting land around the castle to Strata Florida
Abbey. It was the Welsh who destroyed the castle around 1190, when the
local princes of Maelienydd finally resorted to violence against what they
saw as Rhys' incursion into their ancestral lands. Rhys tried but failed to
restore his presence in the area four years later, after which the castle
seems to have been left to moulder away. However, some reports suggest
that the ruins of the tower on the motte were used to house a battery of
guns during the Civil War. The site of this castle has now vanished. It probably lay somewhere between the church of St Bride and the river, when the
river took a more sinuous course directly below the churchyard and the motte.

   Around 1200 the Mortimers built a castle comprising a low motte and probably a rectangular bailey on the eastern bank, and it
is the site of this castle that you can visit. The castle was taken by the Welsh under Llywelyn ab Iorwerth in 1231 after a two-week
siege. In 1307 it was described as simply 'the site of an old castle'. The site of a quarry separates the shelf on which the castle was
built from the area around the church. In 1783 a mass grave was found in the churchyard just north of the castle site when foundations were being dug for a new tower, and many of the skeletons it contained were believed to have been beheaded. Initial reaction
was that these were the bodies of the Mortimer garrison killed when the castle was captured in 1231 (as intimated by the information board at the castle site), but documents suggest that in fact the garrison was allowed to leave unhindered. More likely the
bodies came from some other episode of border or inter-Welsh warfare.

Continue on the road, enter a park and walk down to a children's play area. Here you can choose to cross the footbridge over the Wye and turn right to explore the woods along the river's banks before returning to and recrossing the bridge.

The walk itself turns left just before the bridge and takes the path that runs just above the Wye to join a small street which leads you up to the B4518 which heads out to the Elan Valley. Just before reaching the B4518 you'll pass on your left the Lost Arc, which has a poster detailing some of the building's history, as a woollen mill, a leather workshop, a hall, a cinema and a supermarket before its present incarnation.

❷ Turn right on the B4518 and cross the Wye, then take the first left, to then bear left again down some steps to a park alongside the Wye where you get a good view of the bridge you've just crossed and a series of waterfalls (see the photo on page 26).

From where you entered the park, keep to its right-hand edge and you quickly come to a path that leads out of the park via a small gate. Take this and follow it up to a road, on which you turn left, and then left again at a road junction immediately reached, so you are then walking along a road with the park on your left. Keep right at the first bend.

❸ After about a third of a mile the road bends sharply to the left, but you keep straight on along a wide gravelled track which is signposted as part of the Wye Valley Walk. Shortly before you would reach a collection of farm buildings, you come to a wide 'yard' where there is a junction of many tracks and gateways into fields. You want to take the fourth of five gates on your right so as to then walk down a grassy track between two hedgerows. This will lead you down to a gate, through which you enter a field then follow the hedgerow on your right. You'll pass to the right of a small wood to leave the field through a gate and head down a track, passing first a bungalow on your right and then a large house on your left. Here the track swings right to then pass by some farm buildings on your right.

4 Just before you would reach the B4518 you come to the tarmacked path that forms part of the Elan Valley Trail, a cycleway and footpath. Turn left on this through a small gate, and follow this along till you reach a road. Here you turn right and cross the B4518 to walk along a small road. When you reach an even smaller road off to the right which carries the warning sign 'Unsuitable for wide vehicles', turn right down this, to pass a white-painted house on your left.

5 When this road comes to a T-junction in front of another white-painted house, turn left and follow this road along. The road ends at the entrance to Rhydoldog House, and just yards before the start of this property's drive, you want to take the track off the right, passing another house on your right, and reaching the entrance to

Ty Borth on your left. Here you go through the gate ahead of you (and just to the right of the gate for Ty Borth) to take the track-cum-path up the hillside. This will lead you to a gate which you go through to enter a field, in which you follow the line of the old bank ahead and uphill. This will lead you to a gate which you go through to enter the yard of another white-painted house. Keep the house to your right (and its barns to your left) and walk up to the far end of the house and an outbuilding, to turn right through a gateway onto a track on the wooded hillside.

6 Follow this track, which shadows the field boundary on your right, and it will lead you to a gate in the far right-hand corner of this 'enclosure'. Go through this gate and keep right at the fork in the track soon reached. Keep on the track and in due course you'll start to follow a fence on your left. Where the track bends to the right, go through the gate on your left to enter the top of a slightly overgrown field. Follow the fence on your left, and shortly the track bends to the right and drops downhill with fields to either side. You'll soon reach a large old barn below you; keep to its right to join the gravelled track which serves this farm.

7 Turn right on the track and follow it through woodland and out between fields beyond to meet another track. Turn left on this and follow it along, passing to the right of another farm, till it meets a road. Turn right on the road, cross the stream and turn right at the road junction on the far side. Follow this road along till it meets the B4518. Cross the road and turn left along it and in quick succession you'll come to the entrance to the Elan Valley Trail, a community garden, St Bride's church and the Triangle Inn. Keep following the B4518 to return to the clocktower.

CHURCH OF ST BRIDE, LLANSANTFFRAED CWMDEUDDWR

The present church is the result of a rebuilding in the late 1860s by the architect F.R. Kempson of the former church which had been built in 1778. The original church is thought to have built in the 12th century, and stood to the north of the present site, but it has left little evidence of its existence, even in the documentary record. Rebuilt in 1778, by 1818 it was noted that it resembled a barn – low, long and dark – and had a roof covered in shingles. One suggestion is that the original church formed part of a small monastic settlement which ran up and over the summit of the hill on the road to the Elan valley.

The only item to survive the two rebuildings is the stoup in the porch. This is carved with three simple faces and is of indeterminate date, but early Norman at the latest. The porch is open to visitors, but the church itself is often closed.

Walk 5
St Harmon

5.5 miles on roads, footpaths and tracks. The ascents are very gentle and the views from the ridge you cross very rewarding. There is one small stream you need to ford or step across if longer-legged. You pass through the site of a Roman marching camp and Gilfach Nature Reserve, where, if you time it right, you could stop for a tea break (see page 34).

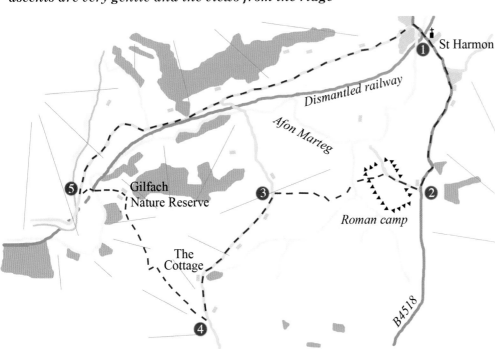

Park near the church in St Harmon.

1 Whilst there is a footpath and small farm lane that can be used to avoid walking on the B4518, at the time of writing up this walk, two stiles were missing on the path which meant clambering over barbed wire fences, so we have, sadly, opted to start this walk down the B road. Thus, walk south on the B road (heading towards Rhayader).

2 After a bit over half a mile you come to a double bend, which you go round to reach a cream- or white-painted cottage on the right, followed by a tarmacked lane.

ST HARMON

St Harmon's monastery was probably founded in the 6th century, and possibly dissolved after 1066. It was a *clas* foundation and developed as the mother church of the region. Its precise site is unknown, though it may have been within the present circular churchyard. Folklore has it that it was founded in 429 on land granted by Vortigern on Waun Marteg north-east of St Harmon and that the saint and his followers initially spent 40 days on the site in prayer for his sins. South of Waun Marteg is a tumulus sometimes called Bedd Garmon and as such is supposed to be where the saint is buried (it also called The Mount, and is named as such on current OS maps). However, Garmon died in 448 at Ravenna in Italy and his body was buried in Auxerre Cathedral. Some now think that a different Garmon was involved with the foundation here, a Breton by the name of Germanus who, in the 700s, spent time in Ireland and Wales before becoming Bishop of the Isle of Man. The settlement was sometimes known as Llanarmon, so when this was translated into English its name became Harmon rather than Garmon, the English not appreciating that the G had been dropped from the Welsh name.

The monastery's church once contained the staff of St Curig 'covered on all sides with gold and silver'. This was believed to have the power to cure tumours and other diseases if a gift of one penny was given in addition to one's prayers, as recorded by Gerald of Wales writing in the 12th century. Other tales speak of people trying to get away with paying half a penny, but the result was that the tumour only subsided in the middle. If the person returned and paid another half penny, the tumour then duly disappeared.

The present church (open in daylight hours between April and September) was built after an earlier one was demolished in 1821. This had been described as long, low and dark, and the new church was built to a smaller floor plan. In turn the new church was extensively refurbished in 1908, with a new chancel, north vestry, and window and door openings, whilst a west gallery was taken out. A bell turret was also built, only to be taken down in the 1930s. The font remains from the Norman church.

Francis Kilvert the diarist was vicar of St Harmon in 1876-7. In May 1876 he described the church as having a 'bare cold squalid interior and high ugly square boxes for seats, a three-decker pulpit and desk, no stove, a flimsy altar rail, a ragged faded altar cloth, a singing gallery with a broken organ, a dark little box for a vestry and a roof in bad repair, admitting the rain.'

The churchyard is one of the most circular examples in Powys, thus indicating an early Celtic foundation. It is also raised, though the drop on the west has been caused in part by the building of the railway line. The broad bank inside the churchyard on the south might be an early feature, and there are references to there once having been a mound to the south-west of the earlier church. Churches dedicated to St Garmon often have such a mound, which is believed to have been used for preaching.

The settlement always seems to have been a small one; the tithe map in the mid 19th century shows a few houses on the south side of the river, and the Sun Inn (now a private house) and a couple of houses on the north side.

Turn right down this lane. As you start walking down the lane, try to ascertain the line of the Roman Camp in the field on the left, for about half way between the start of the lane and the bend ahead, you pass through the edge of the Roman Camp. Continue round the bend, then go through the first field gate on the left. Walk along the field boundary to the end of the field, and pass through a gateway into the next field, still following the field boundary on your right, After a few yards you will leave the area of the Roman Camp.

CWM NANT ROMAN CAMP
Thought to be a marching camp, so only briefly occupied, the south-eastern side is of the greatest prominence and retains, in its centre, the only identifiable entrance. Just 4.5 miles to the west is another similarly sized marching camp at Esgairperfedd. This measures 270m by 235m and has a turf-covered rampart currently 0.4m high and between 2m and 3m wide.

The path still keeps to the right-hand side of this field, but soon leaves it to head down the very grassy line of an old track to a stream which you need to ford or step across. Over the stream, turn half left and head up the far bank to a gate into a field. Go through this, and then follow the field boundary on your right away from the stream; this will lead you to a gate in the far right-hand corner of the field where you join a track. Walk down this track to meet a road.

3 Turn left on the road and follow it along, Having passed a set of old farm buildings on a bend on the right called The Cottage, keep an eye out for the track off to the right in about 500 yards which is signposted for the Wye Valley Walk. This you take.

4 Keep following the track through a few field gateways and keeping to the fenceline on your right and it will lead to the crest of an unexpected ridge, below which lies the valley of the Afon Marteg, with that of the Wye to the half left. Keep following the waymarked path downhill, this heading to the left briefly before turning right and slanting downhill. You will eventually come to a double gate and a welcome sign for the Gilfach Nature Reserve. Through the gates, keep on the track which now follows a field boundary on your left and you will come to the Nature Reserve's largely stone-built but partially timber-framed Visitor Centre on the left.

Just past the first building, go down the path and enter the yard between the buildings. If open, you may wish to visit the centre. Your route turns left in the yard and takes the access road that serves the centre, following it as it turns right and heads down first across the line of the old Mid Wales Railway and then the Afon Marteg to meet a road.

GILFACH NATURE RESERVE

Gilfach is a hill farm managed organically and for the benefit of wildlife by the Radnorshire Wildlife Trust. The reserve's Education and Visitor Centre has been created from the barn which stood opposite the farmhouse. Nest boxes are fitted with cameras and there is pre-recorded footage of other wildlife activity by animals such as badgers. There is a gift shop and café, for those who want to pause en route; bear in mind this is only open (at time of going to print in 2016) from Monday to Friday between 10am and 5pm during the months of April to September, and also on weekends during April, July and August and at school half terms.

The house at Gilfach was originally a peasant hall house, consisting of a larger bay at one end, separated by a through passage from the hall and a smaller bay at the other end. Inside the stone wall, crucks supported the roof structure. It is not known when it was originally built; tree-ring dating proved unsuccessful. In about 1550 it seems to have been somewhat reconfigured, then, around 1600, a large stone fireplace was erected in the hall and the larger bay became a cow-house. In about 1700 an upper parlour wing was added, distinguished by a gabled dormer with decorative timber framing which you pass as you approach the building down the hill.

The walk can be extended on nature trails around the farm, including one down the valley of the Marteg to its confluence with the Wye.

5 Turn right on the road and this will lead you back to St Harmon, following the line of the railway to your right. When you reach the B road turn right to return to the church.

MID WALES RAILWAY

Parliamentary approval was granted in 1859 for a railway line that was to run from Llanidloes to Llandovery, via St Harmon, Rhayader, Newbridge-on-Wye, Builth Road and Three Cocks junction, from where its course lay along what had originally been part of the Hay Railway. Work on the line formally began on 2 September 1859 with the cutting of the first sod, but further work on the 46.7 mile line was delayed until 1862. The line to Three Cocks from Llanidloes was opened to goods traffic on 1 September 1864, and to passengers on 21 September 1864. The intention was to extend the line from Llanidloes via Llangurig and Strata Florida to Aberystwyth, but this was never built apart from the section to Llangurig.

On 1st April 1888 control of the line passed from the Mid Wales Railways to the Cambrian Railways Company, and in the following year the Welsh Railways Through Traffic Act formally created the Mid Wales Line. This went from south Wales to Cheshire and formed an alternative route to that via Newport, Abergavenny, Hereford and Shrewsbury, a route that survives to this day. In practice the Mid Wales Line never received substantial use, and what use it had was almost entirely goods traffic.

During the First World War all goods and passenger traffic was stopped on the line so that it could be used solely by trains carrying coal from the south Wales coalfield to Scapa Flow in the Orkneys, the main home base of the Royal Navy. These trains became known as Jellicoe Specials after Admiral of the Fleet John Jellicoe.

The line returned to normal use after the war, but was then closed to passenger traffic in 1962, part of the line still being used for freight up until 1967.

Walk 6
Llananno, Tinboeth and Moelfre

7 miles largely on a mixture of footpaths, quiet roads (apart from one short section of A road) and tracks. There are only a couple of stiles, but one is quite awkward. The walk is set in rolling country with one steep section of quiet road to climb and a more gentle walk up to Tinboeth Castle. There are several good viewpoints. You may be able to obtain sustenance from a lay-by café near Llananno church.

To the north of Llanbister on the A483, and just to the north of Llananno church, prominent signs point to the east (to the right if heading north) for a WC, Telephone and Picnic Site, together with a brown sign indicating an information point. Park in the small car park by the toilet block.

❶ The walk starts by heading on up the small road alongside the car park to a T-junction, where you turn left. Walk up this road, ignoring a road off to the right.

❷ Just past the crest of the hill, take the track off to the left past a new house.Go through the gate into a field and keep on the track alongside the field boundary on your left. At the far end of the field, turn off the track to the right and walk up a short grassy stretch to a gateway. Go

through this, and follow the field boundary on your right to another gateway. Here you want to look out for the small lump of stonework on the horizon off to the left, for that marks the site of Castell Tinboeth. Go through the gateway and continue following the field boundary on your right to the next gateway.

③ Through the gateway the path turns right, but the farmer has created a permissive path up to Castell Tinboeth off to the left, which may or may not be open to use. If it is, it's worth following it up to the castle site: the only standing stonework left of a castle in Radnorshire (however slight!), some impressive earthworks, fine views in the right weather, and a rustic picnic table on the way up. Having visited the site, return to this point and keep following the 'main' footpath, making its turn to the right and keeping following the field boundary on your right.

Go through the gateway at the end of the field, cross a track, and again follow the field boundary along on your right. In the far corner of this field you need to drop down to cross a stream, then head up the far bank to the corner of the field where you cross the remnants of a stile into the next field. Once again keep following the field boundary on your right, quickly joining a track. Shortly before this track reaches the gate to the next field, look out for a gate on your right. Go through this and walk up and across this field, paralleling the field boundary on your left, to a gate on its far side, through which you pass to join a road.

CASTELL TINBOETH

The castle was built by the Mortimers by 1282; it was known as 'Dynbaud' and was garrisoned by 5 horsemen and 30 foot soldiers during the period that led up to the death of Llywelyn ap Gruffudd (see under Walk 23, Aberedw); it is not mentioned prior to this date. The name might derive from 'Din-baud', or Maud's fort, referring to Matilda de Braose, the wife of Roger (III) Mortimer (d.1282) and a formidable lady. An earlier prehistoric hillfort, Welsh or Norman castle might have crowned the site. The castle was still in use in 1316 and was handed over to Edward II in 1322 along with other Mortimer possessions after Roger (IV) Mortimer's rebellion. This is the last mention of the castle, and with no town near the site, it probably soon fell into decay.

A small polygonal ward was surrounded by a stone wall, on the south-eastern side of which was the entrance, probably a double D-towered gatehouse in the Edwardian style. Immediately to the north of the gatehouse are the robbed-out remains of what might have been a small circular keep. No other towers appear to have been built along the wall, making for a primitive castle of that date. Outside of the gatehouse lay a small barbican. The three deep gullies to the south of the site may have been formed when quarrying rock from which to build the castle.

MOELFRE CITY

Some ratepayers looked favourably upon their poorer neighbours taking up squatter's rights on the edge of commons, as it could reduce the burden on the parish poor rate. To successfully squat, the occupiers had to build a house in the course of one night and have smoke rising from the hearth by dawn. Such a house was almost invariably built of turves, and the occupiers would subsequently enclose an acre or so of ground on which to help eke out a living. Sometimes freeholders, who lost areas of grazing through the formations of such homesteads, would combine and go and pull the houses down; in some areas this was considered legal if the houses had stood for less than 20 years. At other times, the squatters would eventually manage to replace their house of turf with one of stone, the completion of which would be a cause of great celebration.

In the late 18th century and early 19th century, many farms in the valleys were being amalgamated, so reducing the number of houses available for occupation. This led potential squatters to combine forces and build a number of houses in well out of the way areas of common, not along their edges. The resulting settlements were given colourful names; Moelfre City is one such. These settlements often provided a home to many of the area's craftsmen, such as basket makers, tailors and weavers. The names given to the houses were generally in English, and characteristically rustic.

4 Turn left on the road and right at the junction ahead. The road will then crest a ridge, drop steeply down to cross a stream, then rise to crest another ridge.

5 Just over this second ridge, take the wide track off to the right which is marked as the entrance to Green Cottage. Having gone through one gateway, take the right fork (i.e. not that to Green Cottage which goes straight ahead at this point) and follow it as it zig-zags its way down towards a yellow-painted bungalow and stables. About 60 yards before you reach the bungalow, go through the small gate in the railed fence on your right and then walk across to the corner of the paddock right by the bungalow. Here you will find a stile which you cross to then take a steep path down to a footbridge across the stream, then head up the bank the other side. When at the top of the bank, head across the field you find yourself in, heading slightly downhill to cross a little stream by a 'bridge'. Head across the rest of the field to the gate that's in the far hedgerow (not the gate at the right-hand end of the hedgerow). Passing through this you'll find yourself on a track which you follow down to a gate out onto a road.

CHURCH OF ST ANNO, LLANANNO

The early history of the church is unknown, and it is not even mentioned in surviving documents of 1291 or 1535 which detail the other churches in Radnorshire. Even the name of the saint to whom the church is dedicated – St Anno – is obscure, not even the saint's sex being certain. However, the fact that the dedication was not altered to Anne, and the church's position close to the river, both suggest that this was the site of an early church.

In 1851 the west end was used for a school. An account of 1874 suggests that some restoration had taken place before the church was taken down in its entirety in 1876, the timbers forming the screen put into store, and a new church built using some of the old stone to form the internal face of the walls. The screen was reinstalled three years after the church had been rebuilt, at one fifth of what it had cost to rebuild the church.

The screen, the work of the Newtown School of screen-carvers, is arguably considered 'the finest piece of substantially complete church screenwork remaining in Wales'. The current church is wider than the earlier, as shown by the lengthening of the screen and loft to fit the new. The tracery heads in the bays to either side of the doorway are of six different designs, carved on both faces. The head beam above the arches has a leaf and flower trail carved along its length on its western face, and what has been described as 'probably the finest rendering of the water plant as a decorative motive in existence' on its eastern face. Panels of many different designs then arch under the rood loft to the bressumer at the front foot of the loft. A Wyvern at the southern end of this bressumer disgorges a vine trail, with a pomegranate trail below. The west-facing parapet of the loft has 25 canopied niches separated by pinnacled buttresses. The saints in these niches were only carved c.1880 (the screen itself dates from the early 1500s). Traces of paint have been found on the earlier woodwork, suggesting that this was once richly painted.

6 Turn right on the road. After about two-thirds of a mile you'll meet your outward route: turn left at the first road junction and right at the next to walk back down to where you parked.

However, the walk continues to Llananno Church. Continue to the main road and cross it; then walk along the large layby to the far end. Turn through the gateway onto the track to Glanrafon Farm and then take the track off to the left to visit the church. Having seen the church, return along the main road to your car.

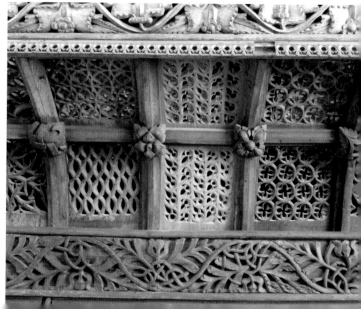

Walk 7
Felindre and
Castell y Blaidd

8 miles largely on tracks which were once drovers'
roads. If you choose gates rather than adjacent
stiles, you can make the walk stile-free. Set in rolling
countryside but with no steep ascents or descents.
Your destination is the rarely visited Castell y
Blaidd and its surrounding landscape with a
tumulus and an old settlement site.

Park near the crossroads on the B4355 to the north-west
of the pub (i.e. in the direction of Newtown) in Felindre.

For a large part of the walk (until you start the return
from Castell y Blaidd) you will be following Glyndwr's
Way, so keeping an eye out for the white acorn sign of a
long distance path, or the dragon symbol for Glyndwr's
Way can provide added pointers to the directions in this
description.

❶ Walk down the road heading south-west from the
crossroads (signposted to Llanbister). Immediately past
the farm on your right, go through the first gate (there
is a sign for Glyndwr's Way on the left of the road at
this point) and walk up past the barns and then the
farmhouse. Glyndwr's Way keeps to the track which
turns right at the end of the farm and then swings
left and heads up the hill, passing through field gates
between one field and the next to follow the line of the
ridge up the top of the hill. At times the track is very

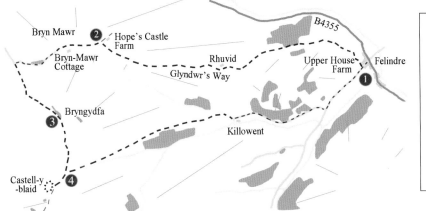

GLYNDWR'S WAY
This 135 mile long distance path was designated a
national trail in 2000, to mark the millennium. It runs
from Knighton north-westwards to Machynlleth,
thence north-eastwards to Welshpool, and links
various places connected to Owain Glyndwr. It has a
reputation of being quite a hard route, with limited
towns and villages to rest up in, but can be walked in
9 days of distances varying between roughly 13 and
18 miles.

DROVERS' ROADS

Drovers' roads probably go back to the ancient trackways such as the Kerry Ridgeway that followed the ridges of the hills running through Wales. These routes would have been above the marshy valley bottoms with firmer ground for cattle and sheep, making ideal routes for those moving stock. Other tracks would have been developed through the movement of cattle and sheep between lower ground in winter and higher ground in summer. As markets and fairs developed in the Middle Ages routes would have been created to and from the towns where these were held. As towns and cities grew with the coming of the Industrial Revolution, such places became new or enlarged foci for the gathering in of fatstock ready for slaughter. It is this period that saw the greatest use of what are now termed drovers' roads, the routes gradually shortening as the railway network edged westwards, with the foci then becoming stations that had stock handling pens.

Many of the open tracks on the ridges leading out of central Wales made ideal drove routes: they often passed through unenclosed land, they avoided the growth of turnpike roads with their tolls in the valleys, and they provided firm footing for man and beasts, but not the firmness of a turnpike road that, over a distance, could cause lameness in beasts of the hillside and field.

New inns opened that could offer a field for holding livestock overnight and beer and sustenance to the drovers, though possibly only the head drover would sleep in the inn, the rest bedding down in the field. The head drover was often a man of business who also used his journeys to carry money and orders from the places he passed through to individuals and businesses in the town or city of his destination. To save the risk of carrying too much cash, often the money was paid over from the sale of stock, and drovers became responsible for founding several banks in which they lodged the money given them at the start of their journey. In this way was founded the Bank of the Black Ox which was to become Lloyds Bank (with its current sign of a black horse).

Some of the drovers' inns would have smiths who could shoe cattle if they were going lame or before they took to hard road surfaces (each cow would require eight shoes due to their cloven feet). The inns also got to know the drovers' dogs, often corgis, for when the drovers reached their destination, they would often need to spend some days there selling the stock and dealing with their other business, and sometimes the dogs would make their way home of their own accord, stopping at the inns for food en route, the drovers settling up for the dogs' food bill on their next visit.

Many of the drovers' roads in central Wales had fallen out of use by the late 1800s.

obvious, at others less so, but there is often a sunken way if no track, and the remains of a hedge bank on your right. As you near the crest of the hill, you pass alongside a wood on your right. Once over the crest, the track turns slightly left (ignore one off to the right) and passes through a field gate to join a prominent track, hedged on both sides. Follow this ahead (ignoring a turning off to the left) down into a small valley where you pass through a farmyard, passing the farmhouse on your left and barns to your right.

Continue on an obvious track which swings right and then left up the next hillside, passing a small triangular copse on your left. The track, which becomes more grassy underfoot, passes through a succession of field gates, always keeping to a fence on your left, then goes by the remains of a stand of Scots pines to meet another track near Hope's Castle Farm. You turn right on this and then almost immediately meet a tarmacked lane that serves the farm.

2 Turn left on this and follow it down into the next valley. Here the lane turns sharp right, but you turn left, initially on a stony track off which you almost immediately turn to keep straight ahead on a grassy track which heads uphill (the stony track bearing off to the right and following the valley). The track passes by a pond hidden in trees on the right then heads towards the remnants of a stand of larches and Scots pines, passing through a gate or over an adjacent stile into the wood, heading briefly up the wood's far side, then passing back through the wood to another gate and adjacent stile.

3 Once through the gate or over the stile you turn left to initially follow the fence on your left, but after some 30 yards head more out into the field to soon see a wide wooden bridge across a small stream. Head for the bridge and cross it. You then cross the field roughly on the line of the bridge to a gate into the next field. Once through this you turn slightly right and head towards the left-hand slope of a small thimble-like hill just ahead – you should also see two wooden marker posts setting out the line of the path. You cross a stony track and head up the side of the hill to see the earthworks of Castell y Blaidd ahead of you on a second peak of the hill. From Castell y Blaidd you can see the almost circular settlement site, marked out by a bank on the upslope further ahead.

CASTELL Y BLAIDD, 'CASTLE OF THE WOLF'

The origins of this site are obscure. The earthwork is a roughly horseshoe-shaped single rampart and ditch on a low hill, and might have been a prehistoric enclosure – but possibly not a hillfort as such as one side was not built – or the site of a medieval castle that was not completed. If it was the site of an early 13th-century castle built by the Mortimers, then it may have been abandoned for the better sited Tinboeth (see Walk 6), visible a mile away to the south-west. Some consider that the name Blaidd (Wolf) is derived from the name or nickname of the original owner of the site who fought the Saxons in 617.

To the north, on the slight ridge you have just crossed, is a tumulus. Some 285m to the south-west, on the other side of a small valley, are the low almost circular earthworks of what are thought to represent building platforms of a former settlement (shown in the centre of the photograph below), but whether the two sites are in any way related is also unknown.

4 Return to the stoned track, on which you turn right and then essentially keep straight ahead till you reach Killowent Farm. This means not following the main track when it bends to the right to head to a set of new barns, but keeping to a grassier track which shadows the valley on your right. At Killowent Farm you join a tarmacked lane which you follow to a T-junction. Turn left and walk back to the crossroads where you parked.

Walk 8
Knucklas

6 miles on a mixture of footpaths, quiet roads and tracks. The outward journey has a couple of climbs (one to the site of Knucklas Castle), neither too long or arduous, and one steepish descent. There is the occasional stile. The return route is via a quiet and only gently undulating road. For refreshment, there are pubs in Knucklas and Lloyney (to which you can make a detour from the walk).

Park near the Castle Inn in Knucklas.

1 Looking at the front of the inn, walk down the road to its right. At the fork ahead, turn right over a bridge, and then immediately left up a no through road. Carry on along this, passing the Victorian railway viaduct on your left.

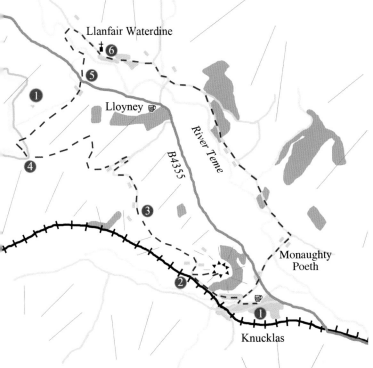

KNUCKLAS VIADUCT

Knucklas Viaduct was built by the Central Wales Railway Company to carry the line constructed between Knighton and Llandrindod Wells between 1860 and 1865, the 190-yard long viaduct being built between 1860 and 1863. The company's chief engineer was Henry Robertson, who is therefore generally credited with the viaduct's design. It is said that the towers and crenellations resulted from the influence of the then owner of the remains of Knucklas Castle, who insisted that if stone from the castle remains was used in the construction of the viaduct, then the viaduct must include some of the features of a castle. When maintenance work was carried out on the viaduct in 2010, evidence was found that stone from the castle site was indeed used to form the viaduct's core.

KNUCKLAS CASTLE COMMUNITY LAND PROJECT

The site of the castle and a total of 21 acres of the hill on which it stands have been bought by some philanthropic locals who are leasing it to Knucklas Castle Community Land Project whilst the money is raised to purchase the site for the whole community, the money being raised through the sale of shares and by donations.

The project involves the creation of allotments (some 35 to date), a community orchard (with 80 fruit trees of many varieties, including cider apples and perry pears) and management of broadleaf woodland, along with looking after the ancient monument. The hope is to create a more self-sufficient village, not just in terms of food supply, but by also having space in which to play and learn skills and the need to co-operate.

2 When the lane turns right, take the path off to the right that leads back on yourself but up the hillside. This will lead you out on to the site of Knucklas Castle.

KNUCKLAS CASTLE

The English variant of the name is derived from the Welsh Cwnc glas, meaning green hill.

A possible hillfort preceded the castle and folklore tells that King Arthur's Guinevere came from Knucklas Castle where lived her father, the giant Gogyrfan according to Welsh mythology. One of the gods of the underworld, his name is derived from *ocur fran,* or evil raven, a bird of ill omen. Claims are also made for the hillfort at Old Oswestry being Gogyrfan's home, whilst the Arthurian legend itself gives King Leo(n)degrance as Guinevere's father.

The castle was built by the Mortimers and completed in 1242, but just 20 years later it was surrendered without a fight to Llywelyn ap Gruffudd. If destroyed by Llywelyn, it must have been rebuilt, for it was fortified in the wars of 1282-83 which saw the death of Llywelyn. It was probably left to decay thereafter, and is not mentioned in accounts of the wars with Owain Glyndwr in the early 1400s.

The castle comprised a small walled enclosure some 15m square, at each corner of which was a round tower, with the main quarters against the eastern wall. To the west was a possible barbican, though the area has been confused by later quarrying. The site is now topped by a sculpture called The Dragon's Tooth, carved by Rolf Hook originally for a Knucklas Castle sculpture trail in 2011; he feels that trees are the silent witnesses of time.

There may well have been a settlement here once the castle was built, but it no doubt suffered in 1262 and again in the early 1400s. By 1536, however, it was one of five Radnorshire boroughs returning a joint MP to Parliament and in the 1830s it was still under the control of bailiffs and burgesses, and had its own court house, even though there were only some 12 dwellings.

Return down the path to the lane, on which you turn right. This will lead you past a house on the right; keep ahead on a smaller track when the lane-now-cum-track bends to the left. The track you're on will itself soon bend to the left and enter a field by a gate. Walk across this field, shadowing the field boundary on your left, to a gate on the far side. This will lead you onto another track, on which you turn right to carry on straight ahead up on to a ridge. You keep following the track and it will gain a gravelled surface and lead you down to a T-junction of tracks and a metalled lane near some farm buildings.

3 Turn right onto the metalled lane and follow it along. After it has passed below a house, make a hairpin turn left onto another metalled lane that leads back above the house, then past some more houses to a crossroads with some tracks. Here you turn right, and take the track that leads for a short distance straight up the slope, then swings left round the bottom of a small quarry and then right and slants up and across the slope to meet another track near the crest of the ridge. Here you turn left to walk on up the line of the ridge. The track in due course meets a corner of fence, which you follow on your left and enter an area of common through a field gate.

4 Once on the common, take the lower path off to the right which slants slightly downhill, at the same time diverging from the fence to the right. As the track nears a single small tree on the left and another stretch of fence

on the right, look out for a small path off to the right. Take this and shadow the fence that is now on your left down to a gate in a corner of the common.

Go through this gate, then turn left sharply downhill, following the gully on your left. This will take you through another gate into a field, where you follow an old sunken track down to the farm at the bottom of the hill. The bridleway heads through several gateways and crosses a small farmyard, keeping close to a stream on your left and passing the farmhouse and a semi-converted barn to your right (but all other barns to your left). This will lead to an old wooden gate out onto the B4355.

5 Cross the B road and enter the field on the far side via a makeshift stile. The path then heads to the far left-hand corner of the field, where you pass through the left-hand of the two gates to then follow the river bank on your right till you reach a footbridge across the Teme. Cross this and turn left on a track and walk up to a road, on which you turn right. Walk along this, visiting Llanfair Waterdine Church on your left.

6 Continue along the road, past what was the Red Lion Inn on your right, now a restaurant also offering accommodation. Ignore the first turning to your left, but take the second, so staying on the left bank of the Teme, unless you want to visit the Lloyney Inn in Lloyney. Take the next turning to the right and pass by Monaughty Poeth to

reach the B road. Cross this and follow the lane back into Knucklas and to the Castle Inn.

THE OLD RED LION INN
Now called The Waterdine, the inn describes itself as a restaurant with rooms, and offers bed and breakfast. The restaurant is only open on certain evenings of the week and for Sunday lunch; it no longer acts as a pub, so you can't just drop in for a drink. Believed to have been built in 1570 as a farm longhouse, it became a drovers' inn on the route down the Teme valley; stock could be penned overnight on its farmland across the road. A thatched barn was also used to hold dances, a local gypsy family often providing the music. The barn was demolished in the 1940s and its timbers used to restore the inn.

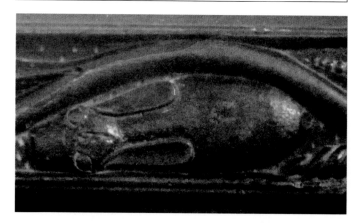

DAVIES TOMBS

To the right of the porch to the church stand a number of tombs of the Davies family, though many of the inscriptions have weathered beyond legibility. One is said to be that of Andrew Davies (d.1780) and bore a carving of two birds that may have resembled a dove and a raven, which has led to a belief that this could have been the tomb of a man also known as Davies Sirevan who was said to always be able to outwit the devil. For example, Davies told the devil that he could not run as fast as a hedgehog, a challenge that the devil couldn't fail to accept. In order that the hedgehog knew which way to go, the race was held along two furrows in a ploughed field; but what the devil did not know was that Davies had two hedgehogs, one for each of end of the hedgehog's furrow. Thus every time the devil reached the end of his furrow, he supposed that the hedgehog had got there before him. Eventually, worn out, he gave up. When Davies was dying, he asked that, when dead, his heart should be placed on a dunghill where, he prophesied, a raven and a dove would fight over it. If the dove won, his friends knew that he would be going to heaven, but if the raven, then to hell. The dove won, and so his friends knew that Davies, not the devil, had had the last laugh.

LLANFAIR WATERDINE CHURCH

The church was completely rebuilt in 1853, when the 11th-century church with its reportedly beautifully carved oak pillars, box pews and roof timbers was knocked down. The current building was designed by Thomas Nicholson, the then diocesan architect for Hereford. The pews each carry the name of a farm in the parish, whilst the communion rail has been made from timbers taken from the Perpendicular rood screen. In the chancel hangs the flag chosen by Lord Hunt of Llanfair Waterdine when he was made a Knight of the Garter in 1979. Lord Hunt was the leader of the 1953 Everest expedition which put Edmund Hillary and Tenzing Norgay on the summit.

Walk 9
Knighton

6 miles on footpaths and roads (that out of the town being quiet). There are no stiles. The walk explores the town and also takes in a section of Offa's Dyke, with a fairly long ascent out of the town.

Park near the Offa's Dyke Centre. (This is worth a visit if you have the time before or after the walk.)

❶ You start the walk on a short section of Offa's Dyke Path. Walk down the well-surfaced path to the rear of the centre, down some steps, then across a small meadow and down to the banks of the River Teme. Here you turn left and in a few yards leave Wales and enter England, even though you're heading west; the joys of the English/Welsh border! Keep following the banks of the Teme and you'll come to a footbridge which you take across the river, just this side of a bridge that carries the Central Wales railway line. Cross the railway line with care, and follow the footpath through a small meadow out onto a road.

❷ Here you leave the Offa's Dyke footpath for the moment (you'll be walking on another section on the south side of the town), and turn right on the road. Walk along this to a T-junction, where you turn right back across the railway and then river.

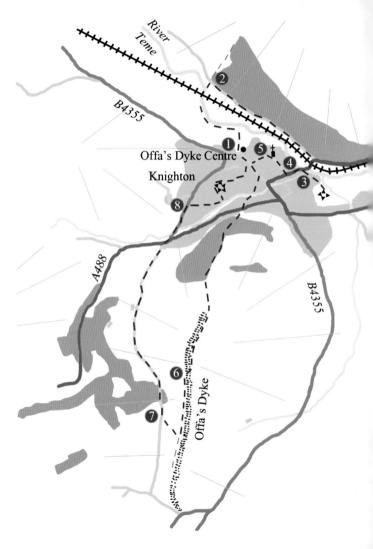

THE LINE BEHIND IS THE EXACT BORDER BETWEEN WALES AND ENGLAND

PLEASE PLACE YOUR FEET IN TWO SEPARATE COUNTRIES

③ If you want to see the site of Knighton's first castle, immediately after you've crossed the river, take the little lane-cum-track off to the left, which will soon lead you through a gate into a field. Take the right-hand of the two tracks and you'll see (more clearly in winter than in summer) the motte of the castle lying just behind a series of buildings on your right. When satisfied, return back down the lane-cum-track to the road, and turn left.

KNIGHTON CASTLE

There are two castle sites in the town, one at Bryn y Castell on the east of the town towards the river, and one at the highest point in the middle of the town, now surrounded and encroached upon by houses. (The fire station has been built into part of the motte.) It was probably this castle that was founded first, sometime before 1086 by Hugh L'Asne ('the Donkey'), and then inherited by the Chandos family, a castle which seems to have been run in consort with that at Norton, 3 miles to the south-east. After the rebellion of Roger Chandos against Henry II in 1186, these two castles were taken into royal hands. Ownership seems to have become complicated in the early 1190s with competing claims by the de Braose, Mortimer, Clifford and de Say families, with the de Braoses having the upper hand by the early 1200s. However, in the troubles between de Braose and King John, the latter demanded the castles back and passed them to the Mortimers, only to almost immediately ask Mortimer to hand them to Robert Sineford, the bailiff of Thomas Erdington, the then sheriff of Shropshire. De Braose attacked the castles in 1208, but Erdington held out. In 1215, the de Braoses, with the help of Llywelyn ab Iorwerth, tried again and this time took both Norton and Knighton castles.

With Llywelyn now established so close to the Mortimer base at Wigmore, the Mortimers did a deal with Erdington and swapped some land in Hampshire for the two castles. With neither in their hands, it is believed that it was they who then encouraged the construction of Bryn y Castell c.1215, committing the defence of the Teme valley to Brian de Brampton. It was probably he who built the large motte here on which a shell keep might have been built, with a possible bailey to the south. The site was probably abandoned when the Mortimers regained Knighton Castle in 1231 (through Ralph Mortimer's marriage to Llywelyn's daughter, part of the dowry being Knighton and Norton castles) and began its rebuilding. The 4m-high motte of this castle at the top of the town remains, but there is no evidence that a stone castle was ever constructed, though stone walls were reported as being visible on the inside of the bailey ditch in 1859, the bailey lying to the south of the castle and now not possible to discern. However, as it appears that Norton Castle may well have had a stone tower added in the 1230s (see page 80), it would seem likely that stone defences would have been added to the more important castle at Knighton. Any stone present in the castle structure may have been reused in the subsequent construction and refurbishment of the surrounding houses. The castle was partially destroyed by the Welsh in 1260, and in 1262, near the height of the power of Llywelyn ap Gruffudd, the remains of both castles were surrendered to the Welsh who probably completed their destruction.

THE ALMSHOUSES
Four almshouses were built in the emerging Arts and Crafts style by Mrs Margaret Green, the sister of Sir Richard Green Price (for whom see page 83), on land he had provided free of charge after he had demolished, in 1881, a group of six existing smaller almshouses in Wylcwm Street which had become unfit for human habitation.

❹ The route then continues along the road, and you take the first turning off to the right and walk up to the church and almshouses.

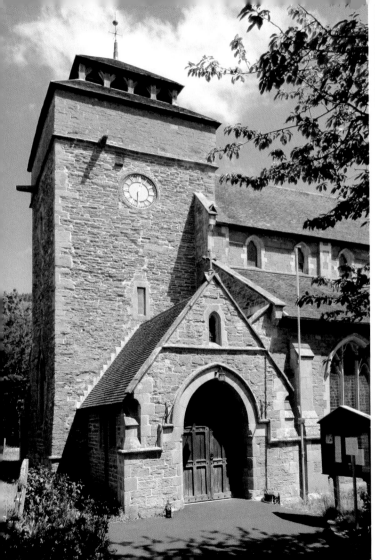

CHURCH OF ST EDWARD

The location of the first church in what became Knighton, and when it was built, remains a mystery. Some suggest that it was on the site of the castle and was rebuilt on the site of the present church when the castle was built, but that would be an unusual location for a newly-built Norman church. The original church may, therefore, have been a Saxon one, all traces of which were lost in a Norman rebuild followed by an almost complete rebuild (excepting the lower parts of the tower) in the 1750s. The church was then dedicated to St Lawrence. By the early 1840s this church, with its private pews, left little space for the population of an expanding town, but it took until 1869 for plans for a new church to be drawn up, and until 1876 before building work started in the early Decorated style to a design by S. Pountney-Smith. This new church was completed in 1897, when the chancel was rebuilt in the Early English style, to a design by J.L. Pearson. This church was dedicated to St Edward the Martyr, a Saxon king killed at Corfe in Dorset in 978.

THE TOWN

Little is known of medieval Knighton, except that it received a charter in 1230 giving it a right to hold a market, and murage grants in 1260 (after the town's devastation by the Welsh) and 1272. As no traces of any stone walls have been found, the 'walls' constructed as a result of these grants probably comprised an earthen bank topped by a wooden palisade. Even then, no indication of their existence remains, apart from tantalising changes in ground level in the occasional location.

Whatever prosperity the town had after the defeat and death of Llywelyn ap Gruffudd in 1282 would have been short-lived, for with deteriorating climate, the Black Death and then the lack of law and order during the rising of Owain Glyndwr, the whole area suffered economically. By the middle of the 15th century Knighton's economy had recovered somewhat, thanks to the wool trade with Flanders and its own small cloth industry. Fortunes ebbed and flowed thereafter, but the prosperous nature of agriculture from the late 1840s led to the construction of a new Butter Cross (demolished within 20 years to make way for a market hall, the original market hall being where the clock tower now stands, the new market hall itself being demolished nigh on 120 years after its construction), a sheep market, a railway and station, the Norton Arms Hotel (now the Knighton Hotel) and the clock tower itself. The latter was given to the town in 1873 on a take it or leave it basis by Thomas Moore, one of the main promoters of the Penybont to Knighton road and of the Knighton and Central Wales railway lines. In the late 1800s industrial development elsewhere and an agricultural slump saw people moving away from the town.

The earliest surviving buildings in the town are the Horse and Jockey inn, its location suggesting a different, earlier layout to the town, and the Old House in the High Street which began its life as a 15th-century hall house. Chandos House, on the corner of the High Street and West Street near the clock tower, was in the 1600s far and away the largest house in Knighton, though now it hardly looks the part. In the early 1800s it was the home of Richard Price before he moved to his newly built Norton Manor (see page 87). It subsequently became the Chandos Arms and was for a while the premier coaching inn in the town. In 1932 part of it was knocked down when West Street was widened.

5 Turn left down Church Street and walk up to the clock tower. Turn left and walk down the High Street until you reach the Knighton Hotel on the right-hand side. Here, go through the archway into the large car park beyond. As you do so, you'll see a road straight ahead of you that you need to take up the hillside to the south of the town; you're back on the Offa's Dyke Path, so its waymarking will also help you over the next section. Head to this road (Larkey Lane) and walk up it, turning right at its top and then immediately left into Ffrydd Terrace. Walk through the gap between the terraces of houses (signposted as the access for numbers 31-42). Turn right in front of the garage block, then take the path off to the left that slants across the hillside. It is from here that you will get the best view of Knighton's second, and bigger, castle site – if you can make it out at the high point of the town.

The path will reach a tarmacked lane which you cross and continue initially up some steps and then through open woodland, to reach a gate out onto Knighton's golf course. The path keeps close to the fence on your right and in due course will come to another gate where you leave the golf course, but keep following field boundaries on your right. Through a further two gates, and always following the field boundaries on your right uphill, Offa's Dyke, which helps form these field boundaries, starts to become more visible. Shortly after going through yet another gate, the line of the path crosses that of the Dyke at a point where the Dyke suddenly becomes much more prominent. (For information on Offa's Dyke, see page 85.)

6 Go through the little gate here and turn left, so that now you are following the Dyke and a fence on your left. The parts of the Dyke that you'll see on this next stretch

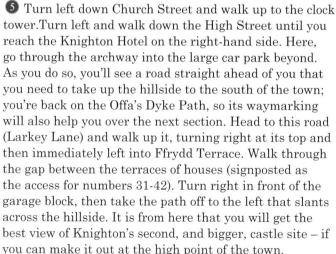

are as grand as you would see on almost any other section of the Dyke. Carry on through two more gates, still following the Dyke on your left, and you'll come to an 'outdent' of a field that leads up to another gate. Turn right just before this, and follow the hedgerow on your left slightly back on yourself and down to a gate onto a road.

7 Turn right on the road and follow it down till it meets the A488. Cross this and walk along Penybont Road till you reach a house on the left called Green Acre. Opposite this, and to the left of a bungalow called Tasley, take the footpath signposted for Glyndwr's Way.

8 Follow the footpath, cross the lane near The Haven and keep heading downhill. Cross another lane and keep on the footpath, with a stream on your right. When you are faced by the grey pebble-dashed wall of a house, take the path slanting uphill to its left. Cross a lane and keep on up the path to reach Castle Road. Here you turn left.

The site of Knighton Castle lies on the ground behind the fire station which you soon pass. You soon meet Market Street, with the Plough Hotel on your left, and here you turn right. Keep ahead to the RAFA building, where you take the right-hand fork, then turn left down The Steppes to reach the Clocktower, with its two nearby cafés. Turn left here to return to the Offa's Dyke Centre, perhaps noticing some strange vehicles that are sometimes parked on the right as you approach it.

The Offa's Dyke Centre is worth a visit to find out more about the Dyke and the local area.

Walk 10
Bleddfa

4 miles on quiet roads, tracks and footpaths, circling a hill called Storling Bank. There are no stiles. The Hundred House inn offers refreshment.

Park near the Hundred House Inn and Bleddfa Church.

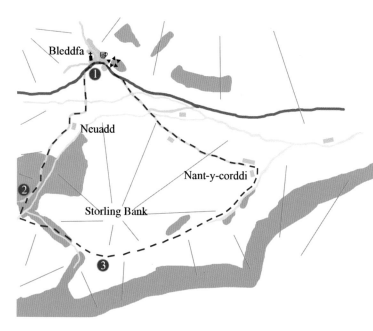

CHURCH OF ST MARY MAGDALENE, BLEDDFA

Traditionally the church was founded by the Irish saint Brendan in the 6th century, but there is no evidence for this. The lancet windows in the south wall of the nave suggest a building date in the 13th century (a church is recorded in 1291), with a roof of the 15th century. The (collapsed) tower has been dated to the 14th century as the result of excavations carried out in 1960-63; the tower was reputedly destroyed by fire by the forces of Owain Glyndwr before the nearby battle of Pilleth (see page 71). The west end of the nave and porch may have been built c.1711. Parts of the chancel and north side of the nave were probably also rebuilt in the early 18th century. In 1818 the box pews were replaced by benches, and flagstones were laid on what had been an earth floor. Restoration was carried out in 1907, with further work in recent decades.

The west end of the nave was formerly a schoolroom, and is now used for an exhibition about the area. The nave and chancel roofs consist of largely original 15th-century timbers, with tie beams, arched-brace trusses and cusped windbraces. In the early 20th century it was reported that many of the timbers had originally carried a simple painted decorative scheme; indeed some red and white paint survives in the chancel. The church was faced with closure in 1973 and in response the Bleddfa Village Church Restoration Society, subsequently the Bleddfa Trust, was formed, and this led to the adaptation of the church interior to allow its use for concerts, exhibitions and other community activities. With the closure of the village school in 1983, the Trust acquired the building and converted it into a gallery and shop. In due course this activity spawned the Bleddfa Centre for the Arts, which now runs courses and hosts talks and exhibitions.

❶ With your back to the church, turn right and walk up the A488, taking the tarmacked lane off to the left at the first corner soon reached. Follow this down and over a stream, past Neuadd farm and then up and along the hillside. Once the lane then starts to slope downhill, watch out for the field gate on the left which leads to a path that keeps to the right of a venerable oak.

❷ Take this path and follow it down and over a bridge across a stream, then up the bank on the far side. At the top of the bank bear left, so that you walk between the valley of the stream on your left and a fence on your right, and in a few yards your route will turn to the right. After

a few hundred yards the path joins a track on which you drop down to cross this stream and then slant up the hillside on the far side. You go through one gateway across the track, after which the track soon swings to the left and then meets a more prominent track.

3 Turn left on this track (to all intents and purposes keeping straight ahead). You'll soon pass a broken stile in the fence on your left. The path technically crosses this and

---

BLEDDFA CASTLE

The castle was probably founded by the lords of Richard's Castle in Herefordshire, who held the surrounding land in 1086 and later held the barony. Succumbing to the Welsh at some point in the 1100s, it was rebuilt in 1195. It fell to the Welsh again in 1262. It was never rebuilt, and in 1304 the dowager lady of Richard's Castle was granted permission to use stone from the castle to build a church tower, and the castle appears to have been abandoned.

The castle mound, now largely obscured by trees and on private ground, was surrounded by a deep ditch and a rampart, partially damaged by later tanning activities associated with the mill, itself first mentioned in 1276. Part of the height of the motte may be due to the collapse of a rectangular keep on its south-western side. The bailey has since been ploughed out, whilst to the south are traces of waterworks which might have been constructed with the partial aim of being able to flood an area of the valley and so help protect the castle.

---

a stile you can probably see in the next fence, but these two fields are nearly always planted with crops and no effort is made to reinstate the paths. It is therefore probably in everyone's best interests just to keep ahead on the track (which the path rejoins further on in any event). Thus, follow the track and it will lead you in a bit under a mile to the farm of Nant-y-corddi.

4 Keep the farmhouse and the first range of barns to your left, then the track swings to the left to leave some poultry houses to your right and gains a tarmacked surface as it heads gently downhill. Keep on this lane, ignoring a turning off to the right, and it will lead you back to the A488, for your best view of the site of Bleddfa Castle. Turn left on the main road to return to Bleddfa, passing Bleddfa Mill in the process.

HUNDRED HOUSE INN

The inn is so called because it was where the Hundred court used to be held, its duties being transferred to the county court in 1867. It had become an inn by 1841 at least.

Walk 11
Pilleth

3.75 miles largely on tracks or tarmacked lanes. There is one steady ascent and a more gradual descent. There are no stiles.

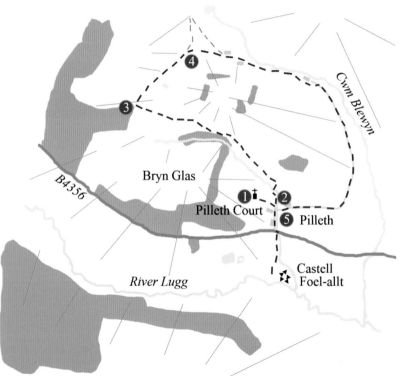

Park at the church in Pilleth, indicated by a sign off the B3456 between Whitton and Monaughty to St Mary's Church and, more prominently, a brown sign to the 'Battle of Pilleth'.

1 From the church car park walk up to the church and pass to its right to head down to a small gate in the corner of the churchyard.

CHURCH OF OUR LADY OF PILLETH

The name Pilleth is derived from the Old English *pyll*, meaning pool, and *hlid*, meaning slope. The manor of Pilleth is recorded in the Domesday Book as Pelelei, but the first record of a church or chapel is in 1198, when it was given by the de Baskerville family to the abbey at Llanthony in the Black Mountains. There is little in the structure to positively date the present building (even the west window tracery has been reset), but it would appear to date from the 14th or 15th century. Whatever structure did exist was burnt during the wars of Owain Glyndwr in the early 1400s, and would have been rebuilt a few years later. (Against the outside of the north wall of the tower is a low wall which ends against a large diagonal buttress at the north-west corner. This is thought to be the remnant of an earlier north wall, and therefore part of the tower destroyed by the Welsh under Glyndwr.) One of the bells is said to date to 1450,

and reports in the mid 1800s noted that the medieval screen survived. The church was much restored in 1872/3 with new windows in the east and south walls, but the church was badly damaged by a fire in 1894 which destroyed all the fittings, though the tower survived. A new scheme of restoration in 1911 lowered the roof line and also took the floors down to their medieval level.

In the years leading up to the Reformation, the church held a wooden statue of the Virgin Mary with a golden crown. This was believed to exert certain curative powers and this, together with the holy well just to the north of the church, made the church the focus of a small pilgrimage site. Five steps lead down into the well, then noted as being large (*y vawr ffynon*); its water was described as being beneficial in curing eye complaints, and cures were also reported for the dumb and the mad.

Earthworks around the church may represent the site of previous dwellings; those behind Pilleth Court might relate to a former orchard or gardens.

Go through this gate and head down the field, aiming for a field gate on the far side on a line to the right of the telegraph pole in the field. On the right is Pilleth Court.

PILLETH COURT

This is a house built of brick (now over painted) on a stone plinth to a U-shape plan. It has a lateral chimneyed hall with an oriel, set between two wings. One of these, rebuilt, contained a parlour, the other a large parlour with the principal staircase. Some later medieval trusses have been reused in the roof. The Court was probably built in about 1556-70 by Stephen Price, brother of James Price of Monaughty, and it was one of the earliest buildings in the area to be constructed of brick.

BATTLE OF PILLETH

In the decades following Edward I's conquest of north-west Wales, the Welsh found not only that they were largely excluded from trade in the new boroughs, which were colonised by English settlers, but also that their lands were milked by their English overlords to fund activity elsewhere in the English realm. Set against that, many individual Welshmen found advancement within that realm, and Owain Glyndwr was one of them, with a career at the Inns of Court in London. At the time of the Welsh uprising he was to later lead, he was aged over forty, and might have preferred a quieter life.

The usurpation of the crown by Henry IV, which broke ties of loyalty to Richard II, and the state of the Crown's finances, which led to an even greater drain on Welsh revenues, were the key causes of the great blaze of the rising. The Crown's inability to deal with the early flames, in part due to the new king's need to not upset those who had supported his usurpation, and the capture of one of Edward I's mightiest castles, Conway, in early 1401 by a small Welsh band, saw those flames spread. A quarrel between Lord Grey of Ruthin and Owain led to the latter joining the uprising. Descended from lines of Welsh princes and with military as well as legal training, he was soon at the head of the revolt. In the summer of 1401 Owain and his forces were on the move around central Wales fanning the embers and, despite some defeats, also notching up victories. In the summer of 1402 Owain led his forces towards the central Marches, and Edmund Mortimer, the acting head of the Mortimer family, his nephew not yet being of age, raised the Herefordshire levies to counter the threat.

Edmund Mortimer is not considered to be one of the more able military commanders of the period, but his captains had a wealth of experience. Owain, however, was fleet of foot in his moves across Wales, often keeping the English guessing as to where and when he would next appear, and an able tactician, using ground to his best advantage.

Why the English chose to advance steeply uphill to attack the Welsh is unknown. Perhaps they wished to strike quickly whilst they knew where Owain was and had the advantage of numbers. It seems that the Welsh withdrew, as planned, as the English advanced, and the English line began to spread out as the more heavily armed soldiers tired: it was the day after midsummer, and no mention is made of adverse weather. But then the Welsh archers in the English army turned and attacked their previous colleagues, in all probability pouring arrows at close range into the English ranks. The Welsh army then charged downhill, possibly aided by some forces hidden up the side valley behind the church, and the advance quickly turned into a rout with probably some 800 killed and Edmund Mortimer taken prisoner. It is said that the bodies were obscenely mutilated by Welsh women, probably the camp followers of Owain's army. The Wellingtonias on the hillside above the church mark the site of where many of those killed were buried.

② Once through the gate, turn left on the tarmacked drive and when it swings to the right carry on along the gravelled track and re-enter the field you've recently been in through a gateway. Keep on the track and almost immediately it bends to the right and you go through a second gateway and cross a 'bridge' over a stream. Keep on the track as it bends left and slants up the hillside. After about half a mile, just after it starts to slope downhill, you turn right onto a grassy bridleway which continues to slant up and across the hillside. Keep on this as it become slightly indistinct and it will lead you to a gate just to the right of a stretch of woodland.

③ Go through this gate and turn right, to follow the grassy track uphill and alongside the fence on your right. You pass through another gateway and keep the fence on your right, but having passed through a further gateway, the track now follows the fence and hedge on your left. After two further gates you will emerge onto a track, on which you turn right, leaving one field between you and some ponds in the valley bottom.

④ This track will lead you past one small farm, but as you near a second farm, the path leaves the track to enter a field by a gate just above a series of barns. Once in the field, keep all the barns to your left and at their far end, between the last one and a line of trees, leave the field by a gate and turn right back on the track. (The path was diverted here a few years ago so you no longer walk through the main farmyard.) The track now has a tarmacked surface and will lead you back in an arc to the farm and buildings below Pilleth Church.

⑤ Where the track splits near the buildings, you can either keep straight ahead and then retrace your steps to the church, or turn left to visit Castell Foel-allt. To do the latter, having turned left, walk down to the main road on which you turn left and then almost immediately right through the first field gate you come to, and where there is the sign for a bridleway. Through the gate, follow the hedgerow on your left and where the hedgerow bends to the left, the bridleway passes to the other side of the remnants of a hedgerow and keeps ahead, staying close to the foot of the earthworks of Castell Foel-allt on your left.

Retrace your steps to the main road. You can then either return to your vehicle along the main road and then up the track to the church, or back to the junction of tarmacked tracks, and turn left to rejoin your outward route and so retrace your steps to the church.

CASTELL FOEL-ALLT

The castle may have been an early Mortimer foundation, giving some protection along a valley that heads out of Wales towards the family's heartland. Its presence is recorded in 1341 when it was the home of the dowager lady of Wigmore. There were two such dowager ladies alive in 1341, Joan de Geneville, the wife of the executed Roger (IV) Mortimer, 1st Earl of March, and Elizabeth de Badlesmere, wife of Roger's son Edmund, who had died in 1331. It was almost certainly the latter who lived here as she had been granted Maelienydd, the Welsh cantref that now forms this part of Radnorshire, as part of her dower. Rubble on the top of the motte and in the ditch certainly suggests the motte once held a tower. The castle is not mentioned in the events of the Battle of Pilleth.

Walk 12
Cascob and Ednol

7 miles largely on tracks (one an old drovers' road) with some quiet roads and footpaths. There are no stiles. There are two steady ascents in quite hilly country, the route offering good views and taking in one church and the ruins of another.

Cascob lies on a no through road off the B4357 to the south of Whitton and west of Presteigne. At the crossroads on the B4357 between Witton and Beggar's Bush, take the turning to the west signposted 'Cascob 2'.

Head along this road, looking out for a lane off to the left, prominently marked with signs for three properties: Cartref, Llwyncelyn and Lower Dyffryn. Keep on the road past this lane and within a few hundred yards you'll come to a wide entrance to a lane off to the right: we suggest parking on the verge at this point and starting

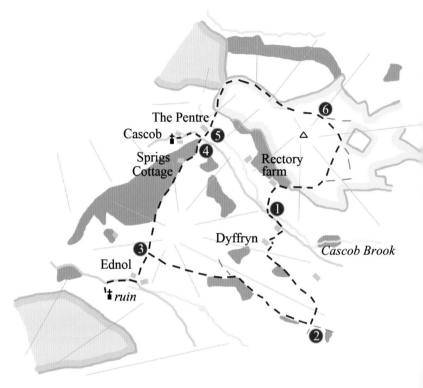

DYFFRYN

The two farmhouses here are both listed buildings, being considered of interest as a pair of farmhouses. The older, formerly timber-framed house dates to the 16th or 17th century and comprises a hall and jettied crosswing, partially rebuilt in stone and with the roof of the hall heightened.

the walk from here as much of the road beyond is very narrow with few options for parking.

❶ Start the walk by walking back along the road to the lane for Cartref, Llwyncelyn and Lower Dyffryn, and turn right up this. Continue up to the farm and turn left in front of the old timber-framed farmhouse, which is in some disrepair (or was at the time of writing anyway), and then almost immediately right up a sunken track that continues straight up the hillside. This soon forks and you bear left, the track soon turning to the left and taking a more gentle approach up the ridge.

❷ When you reach the crest of the ridge you'll meet another track, an old drovers' road (see page 44). Turn

right on this and follow it along, presently passing alongside a wood on your left. At the far end of the wood, go through the gate on the left into a field, and continue alongside the wood, with the line of an old hedgerow on your right. This will lead you to another gate, through which you turn slightly right and cross to another gate which leads out onto a track that runs parallel to and slightly to the left of the crest of the ridge. Keep following the field boundaries on your right, passing through a few gates and past a small wood on your right, and in due course you'll meet a sunken track that crosses your line at right angles at the far end of a field.

3 The circular walk turns right, but to reach the site of Ednol Church, you turn left down the track and follow it down to a road, on which you turn right. When you reach the entrance to Newhouse Farm on the right, take the signposted track off to the left through a field gate. Follow

this up the side of the hedgerow on your right, from which it will then curve away to reach a gate into the next field. Just before it does so, the low stonework remains of Ednol Church lie amongst a group of trees (and nettles in their season) on the left.

EDNOL CHURCH

The name is probably derived from a Saxon personal name, Eada, and the word for wall or well. The church was built as a chapel of ease (for the 'ease' of parishioners being able to get to church) for the parish of Old Radnor. Its community would only ever have been the inhabitants of Ednol farm together with those of a few other farms and cottages in the vicinity, some of which would have stood on the occasional eroded house platform in the field to the west. The remaining walls are some 1m high, but lie under accumulated soil and nettles. The last burial here is said to have taken place in 1829.

Having seen the remains, you can resume the circular walk by returning to the crest of the ridge where you met the sunken track. Follow the sunken track over the ridge and then down the far hillside, its route soon following the edge of a wood on your left. When you reach Sprigs Cottage, the path then follows the cottage's drive down to the road.

④ Turn left on the road, noting the almost immediate turn to the right for The Pentre, and continue along till you reach Cascob Church in a few hundred yards.

CHURCH OF ST MICHAEL AND ALL ANGELS, CASCOB

The church probably dates from the 13th century, the original tower may date to the 14th century, whilst 15th-century work includes the re-set south nave window, the nave roof and probably the porch. The thick walls show evidence of rebuilding. The screen has five bays on either side of the opening, and the lack of carved trails of vine leaves, dragons or other figures often found elsewhere on the bressumer and head beam, indicate that they and the panels in between might have originally been painted, the panels probably with images of saints. The church was all but a ruin in 1887 and was rebuilt in 1895.

The mound around the tower has been considered to be both a prehistoric tumulus and the site of an early if temporary Norman castle motte, but is more likely simply to be the spoil heap from a collapsed and rebuilt church tower. Another low mound south of the porch appears to be formed of debris from a time of restoration.

On a wall in the church is preserved a charm for protection against witchcraft. It reads:

In the name of the father, Son and of the Holy ghost. Amen XXX and in the name of the Lord jesus Christ who will deliver Elizabeth Loyd from all witchcraft and from all evil sprites by the same power as he did cause the blind to see the lame to walke the dum to talke. Pater pater pater noster noster noster ave ave ave Maria in secula seculorum X on X Adonay X Tetragrammaton X Amen and in the name of the Holy Trinity and of Hubert ... Grant that this holy charm Abracadabra may cure they survent Elizabeth Loyd from all evil sprites and all ther desises [?devices]. Amen X X X by Jah Jah Jah.

ABRACADABRA
ABRACADAB
ABRACAD
ABRAC
ABR
AB
A

The belief was that as the lines faded so the threat of witch-craft would disappear.

Having visited the church, return down the road and turn left up the lane to The Pentre.

5 Keep on the track past the various houses on the left and follow it up the hillside till you reach a finger post in a saddle in the ridge. Turn right here, and immediately fork left to take the track on the commonland that stays close to the fenceline on the left. Stay on this track past the first 'summit' and it will lead you to a gate in the next saddle. Through this gate, keep on the track, which now circles round to the left of the second 'summit' and you will reach another finger post.

6 Bear right at this one, and it will lead you down to the corner of some fields somewhat surprisingly sited in the middle of the common. Here, turn right and follow the grassy track which swings slightly left through the low saddle, before bending right and becoming a very definite tractor track slanting fairly steeply down the hillside. Keep on the track and this will lead you to Rectory farm, where you turn left down the track and so join the lane that leads back to where you parked.

Walk 13
Norton and Offa's Dyke

5 miles on a mixture of footpaths (including a section of the Offa's Dyke long distance path), tracks and some quiet road. There are some stiles on the Offa's Dyke path. Set in rolling countryside with fine views from Offa's Dyke, the ascents are fairly gentle.

NORTON AND ITS CASTLE

Norton is one of the few places in Wales mentioned in the Domesday Book, when it was held by one Hugh the Donkey, the nickname a reference to his stubbornness rather than stupidity. The current village has the look of a planned settlement with a regular street layout. For much of the history of the castle site, see the box on Knighton Castle on page 57. The 5m-high motte, damaged when the present B4355 was driven past its base, lies in a garden on one side of the road, with the bailey on the other, the outline of which is visible in the boundaries of various gardens. The bailey partially followed the crest of a natural bank which falls away to a stream. The castle was recorded in 1191 and a masonry tower was probably built on the motte in the 1230s. It was taken by Owain ap Madog on behalf of Llywelyn ap Gruffudd in 1262. Leland recorded a 'litle pilet or turret' on his visit in c.1538, presumably the remains of the tower on the motte.

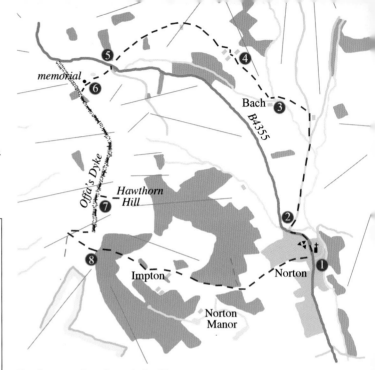

Park near the church in Norton.

❶ Walk along the B4355 towards Knighton (i.e. with the church on the right-hand side of the road). As you crest the rise in the road, the motte of Norton Castle is on your left immediately above the road and just before the driveway to a house. Continue on the road into the valley bottom where you take the narrow tarmacked lane off to the right.

2 Continue along this and after about half a mile cross a stream. Once across the stream the lane rises uphill and you bear left at the fork soon reached. After a few hundred yards you reach some barns set back from the lane on the right, opposite which you go through a gate on the left to enter a field. Make a mental note of where the Victorian farmhouse stands on the horizon of the ridge ahead, for the route of the bridleway which you now follow will, in due course, lead you just to the right of it. For the moment, the bridleway crosses the field and passes through the hedgeline ahead, heading slightly downhill and gently closing in on the stream below and to your left. Once through the hedge, you should see a small wooden gate between the line of the hedge on the far side of the next field and a small coppice further down the hillside. Head to this gate and go through it onto a lane.

the line of an old sunken track through the next field, heading towards a gate in front of some barns to the right of the Victorian farmhouse.

❹ Once through this gate, turn left and then immediately right to pass round the left-hand end of the line of barns, and then take the track that slants uphill, to pass a large new stock barn on your left. Cross the yard by the barn and enter a small field by a gate.

The bridleway now follows the hedgeline on your left to the top left-hand corner of the field, where it turns right in front of a gate and follows the hedge on your left to the far corner of the field, where you leave it by another gate. The bridleway now follows the hedge on your left, passing through more gates to pass by a small barn and coppice on your left. The bridleway keeps following the hedgeline on your left into the first field beyond the barn, and then into the second. Some 30 yards into this second field you want to go through the gate on your left (it is marked with some yellow 'footpath' tape on one of its bars), for from this point the bridleway still follows the same hedge-line, but now to your right.

Follow the hedge along to then pass between a small wood and the hedge into the next field, then keep following the hedge to eventually join the track that slants up the hillside on your left. Turn right on the track and follow it to its junction with the B4355, which is soon reached.

❸ Turn left on the lane and walk down to the stream. Just before the lane crosses the stream to reach the Bach, turn right along the stream bank and cross a footbridge over a tributary. Keep along the stream's bank till you reach a gate into a field on your right. Go through this, then initially follow the line of an old sunken track that heads up through the middle of the field. As you rise up the field you want to head towards its top right-hand corner; more precisely to a gate some 30 or 40 yards to the left of the corner; the Victorian farmhouse should also help as a marker. Go through this gate and again follow

⑤ Cross the B road onto a tarmacked lane, and almost immediately turn right through a gate into a field. Follow the initially semi-stoned track and then grassy 'dingle' below a monument to Richard Green Price. You can clamber up the small hill to have a look; the provision of a bench, albeit in a collapsed state in the early spring of 2016, by the monument does suggest that the landowner takes no exception to your walk passing over the top of the mound on which the monument stands.

⑥ From the monument, or the dingle below it, you want to head for the far right-hand corner of a strip of woodland close by that runs up the hillside. Here you will find a stile that leads on to the Offa's Dyke path, and indeed the remnants of Offa's Dyke itself. Cross the stile and follow the edge of woodland to its far end, where you cross out by another stile.

From here the path follows the clear line of the Dyke, passing through a few small gates, then, at the end of

RICHARD GREEN PRICE MEMORIAL

The memorial commemorates Richard Green Price, who inherited the Norton Manor estate in 1861. He extended the manor, laid out new gardens and terraces, built a new vicarage, housing for his workers, a new school and helped fund the restoration of the church in 1868. He supported local agricultural societies and was involved in developing Knighton – working to improve its sanitation and water supply, and develop its assembly room, sheep market and main hotel – and also Llandrindod Wells as a Spa town. He was an enthusiastic encloser of commonland, whereby he added some 3,500 acres to his estate. He over-invested in local railways, promoting the Knighton and Central Wales line and subsequently that to Presteigne and the extension of the Kington line to New Radnor, losing considerable sums of money in the process. When he died in 1887 members of his family had to downsize to smaller houses in the village, a by-product of which was a surge in employment for local women 'in service'. He was elected as a Liberal MP for the Radnor Boroughs in a by-election in 1863 following the death of Sir George Cornewall Lewis, and in the ensuing elections of 1865 and 1868. He contested but lost the election for the county seat (there were then two constituencies in Radnorshire) in 1874, when he was made a baronet in the dissolution honours, but then won the county seat in 1880, standing down at the election of 1885 due to ill health. He was a keen supporter of Gladstone and his views on Home Rule in Ireland. He died in London in 1897.

another stretch of woodland, enters a field where the Dyke is a much less prominent feature. Part way along the fence on your right which you now follow, you'll come to a small sign which points out that there is a permissive path off to the left up to a small fenced-off enclosure at one of the two summits of Hawthorn Hill (the other lies in the woodland you've just passed). It is worth, on a clear day, heading up to this enclosure as there is a near 360 degree view over the surrounding valleys and hills – and a table at which you could enjoy a picnic.

7 The circular walk continues along the fence-line from the notice point to cross a stile into the next field. As you cross the stile look half left to mark the position of a field gate at the edge of some woodland, for this is where you will be

OFFA'S DYKE

'There was in Mercia in fairly recent times a certain vigorous king called Offa, who terrified all the neighbouring kings and provinces around him, and who had a great dyke built between Wales and Mercia from sea to sea.' So wrote Asser in his *Life of King Alfred* in 893, nearly a hundred years after the Dyke's construction. The comment 'from sea to sea' has bedevilled the Dyke ever since. Presuming the 'seas' to be the north Welsh coast and the Severn Estuary, antiquarians, historians and map makers have linked various dykes together and called the whole 'Offa's Dyke'. But the Dyke can only securely be said to run from near the north Welsh coast to near Kington, and possibly to the Wye to the north-west of Hereford. There is no evidence of any dyke that could form part of a 'sea to sea' structure over a 20-mile stretch in the vicinity of Hereford, and further south an assorted clutch of dykes may have become cobbled together in historians' imaginations to form parts of Offa's structure.

Even the part which can be safely called Offa's Dyke because of a certain uniformity in its form and route across the landscape varies in its structure depending upon the type of soil, the lie of the land and, presumably, the numbers of workmen, their commitment and the skill of the foreman. Originally the V-shaped ditch on the west side was cut about 2 metres deep, and the bank raised to a height some 8 metres above the bottom of the ditch. Sometimes there is a small bank on the outer side of the ditch; this may simply have been created when clearing out debris from the ditch once the Dyke had been constructed, although it does make the ditch deeper and even more of a barrier and so could have been part of the design. The ground was first stripped of its turves, which were placed in the bank as it was constructed to help hold the loose soil together. Turves were also taken from the area behind the Dyke, sometimes creating the false impression that a ditch was also dug on the east of the Dyke. No evidence for any palisade on the Dyke has ever been found, nor 'gateways' through it, the current gaps being modern creations or gaps left for streams and rivers to flow through. Underneath the Dyke, however, have been found small marking out trenches and the occasional post hole, presumably where a stake was hammered into the ground to mark the line of the Dyke.

What was the Dyke's purpose? If we forget 'sea to sea' and look at the evidence of the structure to the north of Hereford, this suggests it was meant as a boundary marker between the kingdom of Mercia as it was in the 790s and that of Powys. It was never constructed to be a defendable line like Hadrian's Wall, but it could have been patrolled to keep an eye out for Welsh raiding parties, and its steep bank and ditch would have hindered rustlers marching away with oxen, cattle and sheep. Yet there is no evidence that the Dyke was ever maintained; the ditch would have started to fill in from the day it was completed. Perhaps its real purpose lies in Offa's attempt to equate himself with the greatest king of his age, Charlemagne. In or shortly before 789, Charlemagne suggested that one of Offa's daughters marry his eldest son, to which Offa responded that that would be acceptable if his own son, Ecgfrith, could marry one of Charlemagne's daughters. This so irked Charlemagne that he closed Frankish ports to English merchants. Could it be that Offa, in his own fit of pique and rage (his character suggests he was capable of both), decided on a project that would mark him out as an equal of Charlemagne, and that this project was the building of Britain's greatest Dyke?

heading in due course. The path, however, turns right along the fence once you've crossed the stile and heads down to the corner of the field. Here you turn not quite back on yourself to take the signposted bridleway back up the hillside to the gate on the edge of the woodland which you hopefully observed whilst crossing the last stile.

8 Through this gate, follow the path down through the woodland and then out into a field. Here the path turns slightly right to shadow a small conifer plantation on your left and follows a track towards some farm buildings. At the junction with the next field, take the smaller gate on the left and then turn half left away from the track to cross the field diagonally to join the stoned track that serves the farm buildings, turning left onto it. As you descend on the track, over to your right you can see Impton and possibly Norton Manor, which is hidden in the valley to your right and only even partially visible in winter when the trees are bare of leaves. Ignore a bridleway that leads off to the left, and stay on the track to meet the B4355 opposite the church, which you may wish to visit.

IMPTON

It is thought that Impton was built c.1471 by Rhys ap Dafydd, who had served as receiver of the lordship of Maelienydd. It was extended c.1542-43 to provide for the then heir of the family, who had married into the wealthy Bradshaw family of merchants in Presteigne, who were busily acquiring monastic properties at the dissolution. (See also the box on Norton Manor.)

NORTON MANOR

This had been a Mortimer property and so passed to the Crown with the accession of Edward, Earl of March as Edward IV in 1461, but passed out of royal hands in the 1500s by grant, for reason unknown, to a William Horne, a member of a wealthy London merchant family. William then sold the manor to John Tamworth who married a sister of Sir Francis Walsingham, Elizabeth I's spymaster. The manor then passed through several hands before being acquired by a branch of the Price family of Knighton, who resided at Impton. In 1838 the family began constructing a new home below Impton, calling it Norton Manor. When, in 1861, the manor passed to Richard Green, a nephew of the previous Price owner, he took the additional surname of Price. Richard Green Price was to expend much money and energy in developing the village and upgrading the Norton Manor estate (see box on page 83). His expenditure broke the family's finances, and in 1892 the manor was sold to Powlett Millbank, brother-in-law of Sir Richard Green Price's heir, Sir Dansey Green Price. The estate was sold twice in quick succession in the 1920s and broken up on the second occasion. Norton Manor became a base for recuperating troops after the Dunkirk evacuation. The house was turned into a 12 bedroomed hotel, but at the time of writing it is once more a private dwelling.

If you carry on through the churchyard, with the church on your left, you can pass out onto the road that runs behind the church and under the banks of the original castle bailey, which gives you a feel for the size and scope of the early castle.

CHURCH OF ST ANDREW, NORTON

It is unknown as to whether the church owes its existence to the presence of a castle, or whether there was a pre-Norman church on the site. The church lies within what was the bailey to the castle, but on the north side of the churchyard there are suggestions that the boundary may have been more curved which would suggest a church history predating the arrival of the castle.

The tower is thought to be of the 17th century, as is probably the western extension of the nave. In the 1800s the pulpit and medieval screen were white-washed, and a gallery was erected in 1834. A major restoration was carried out in 1868 to the design of Sir George Gilbert Scott, though supervised by James Burlinson. If the restoration respected the earlier church, then it would suggest the previous building was erected c.1300; there is certainly some medieval masonry in the nave, though much of the masonry had deteriorated badly and was replaced. The nave and chancel were rebuilt, transepts added, the height of the tower raised, the gallery removed and the screen restored.

A scion of the Glastonbury thorn in the churchyard was reported, in years past, to flower on old Christmas Day (6th January).

Walk 14
Presteigne

7.25 miles on quiet roads, footpaths and some tracks. There are several stiles. The walk explores Presteigne (where there are several inns and tea rooms) and takes you out into the countryside to the north. You may wish to check to check the opening times for Bryan's Ground (see page 96) so that you can include visiting these gardens.

Park near the church.

CHURCH OF ST ANDREW, PRESTEIGNE

The initial church on the site was possibly a small Saxon one, represented by the surviving masonry at the base of the eastern part of the current north aisle, where the stonework is made from small to medium irregular lumps of greyish-brown fine-grained sedimentary rock incorporating some waterworn pebbles. Indeed the settlement probably originated as a small religious community in Saxon times, its original name Presthemede probably deriving from *preost haemed*, 'the household of priests'.

The first Norman church extended the nave of the Saxon building, and might have largely rebuilt a structure damaged by Welsh raids, but the church remained a narrow one, just some 19 feet wide. In around 1200 the church was rebuilt in the Romanesque style with the nave further lengthened and a new south aisle, together with a freestanding tower. In the early 14th century the church took the present form of a central nave with two aisles, connected the tower to the body of the church, and with a larger chancel. In the 15th century the nave was raised with the addition of clerestory, the chancel was further enlarged, the south aisle widened and a lady chapel added to the south of the chancel. The tower was also partially rebuilt, or raised. The church was restored in 1854-55 and again in 1889-91 when the chancel and south aisle screens were commissioned, to the design of the architect J.L. Pearson. Further restoration was carried out in 1927. There are still some fragments of 15th-century stained glass.

From the 13th century to the Reformation, the Augustinian Canons of Wigmore Abbey held the living and were responsible for some of the late medieval developments, including the chancel.

MARY MORGAN

In the graveyard are two memorial stones to Mary Morgan, a young girl hanged for the murder of her bastard child, one recording her date of death and age, with a warning about sinners casting the first stone, and one erected by a friend of the judge who passed sentence on her which speaks of remorse for that act. The two stones stand close to the church porch, facing each other.

In 1804 Mary Morgan was the undercook at Maesllwch Castle near Glasbury, the home of Walter Wilkins, MP for Radnorshire. Here, in secret in her room, she gave birth to a girl on 23 September. Almost immediately she killed the baby by almost severing her head from her body with a kitchen knife, a crime discovered within hours and of which she was found guilty at the inquest two days later. Her trial began at Presteigne the following April, just after she had turned 17 years old. Within four days she was tried, convicted and hanged. Though punishments then were severe, hanging for infanticide had become rare and the speed with which the execution was carried out has given rise to speculation. Was Walter Wilkins the father and did he orchestrate a cover up? Unlikely, as Mary had named another servant as the father and he had accepted paternity before the child was born. The judge in the case, George Hardinge, felt he found 'no religion in her thoughts'

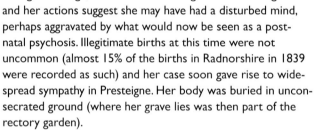

and her actions suggest she may have had a disturbed mind, perhaps aggravated by what would now be seen as a post-natal psychosis. Illegitimate births at this time were not uncommon (almost 15% of the births in Radnorshire in 1839 were recorded as such) and her case soon gave rise to widespread sympathy in Presteigne. Her body was buried in unconsecrated ground (where her grave lies was then part of the rectory garden).

Did Hardinge subsequently have regrets for his actions? The sanctimonious epitaph was erected by the Earl of Ailesbury, a friend of Hardinge's, but what involvement Hardinge had is unknown. A story has it that Hardinge visited the grave on each of his subsequent visits to the town, but is that true? It is unknown who erected the simpler memorial with its warning to sinners, but it is known to have been in place by 1818. Hardinge died in 1816; what would he have made of this second memorial if he knew of its existence?

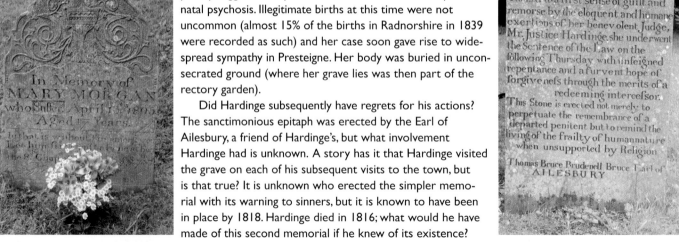

1 From the church, walk along the road that crosses the bridge over the Lugg. Keep on the road, looking out for a stile on the left reached up a few stone steps (and before you come to the end of the run of houses on the right). Once over the stile, cross the field to a point about 150 yards along the hedge from the far left-hand corner of the field, where you'll find another stile. Over this, the path turns fractionally to the right to cross a corner of this next field to another stile. The path may be well visible on the ground, but if not, you want to aim for the mid point between two small conifer woods beyond the field. As you near the edge of the field you should spot a stile just to the right of a stream. Cross the stile, then the stream and walk up the bank. From the top of the bank, you diagonally cross the field, your target being its far corner where a fence meets a hedgerow. Cross the stile here, then the road, followed by a stile into the field on the far side of the road.

2 The path now slants across and up the field, heading towards the left-hand end of the conifer wood at the top of the field, the path passing between the two posts of the nearest electricity pylon. When you reach the wood you walk between it (and the dell it hides) and a hedge on your left, down a finger of the field to a gate. Go through the gate and out onto a road, on which you turn right.

You will follow the road for just over a mile. It soon passes Stocken Farm on the right and its buildings and

duckpond on your left and then heads steeply uphill past a house and converted barn on your right. Further on still, the road goes into the gentlest of dips, where a track leads off to the right to Goat House.

3 Just a few yards before this turning, cross a stile in the hedge on the right. Walk across the field towards the woodland, keeping just to the right of a prominent gully. This will lead you down to the corner of the wood, where you cross a stile, a shallow stream and then keep just to the right of the stream on a path that leads through the

woodland. In due course this will lead you to another stile which you cross to leave the woodland, the path then bearing slightly right to follow a fence on your right, with the stream steeply below you to your left. You soon reach another stile, which you cross to enter a field.

Once in the field, you aim towards the right-hand edge of the collection of buildings that is Willey Hall. As you approach them, keep to the right of a pond and left of a fence to leave the field via a gate just below the farm buildings. Head slightly up the bank beyond the gate, but keep following the fence on your right. Where this bends away to the right you should join the ghost of a track which you keep following ahead and gently downhill. Presently you'll cross a small stream and then see a stile ahead of you in a corner of a fence. Cross this and follow the path on the other side. This will soon lead you gently downhill to meet a wide forestry track.

❹ Turn left on this and after about 100 yards, turn right onto a path that leads through some slightly boggy woodland and then rises up into a dense plantation of firs. Just before you reach a wide ditch not far into the plantation, the path swings left to follow this, to later curve right in front of a fence and leave the woodland near Abley's Green. Cross the track that serves this house, go up the bank on the far side for a few yards, then cross the stile into a field. The path initially stays close to the fence on your left then, when that makes a left-hand turn downhill, carries on round the hillside, always gently descending and staying about 20 yards to the right of a telegraph pole that stands near the lower edge of the field. Near where the field's fence-line makes a turn left to head downhill, you'll pick up a path that initially stays just inside the woodland on the edge of the field, then drops a bit more downhill to cross a stile on the far side of a large holly bush. Keep to the path through the wood, which initially goes slightly uphill then becomes a more obvious path and slants gently downhill. This will lead you down to a gate into a field. Go through the gate and follow the fence on your right downhill (keeping an eye out for the remains of Stapleton Castle on your left) then cross a track and go over a stile into the next field. Keep following the path down, it soon keeping to a field

STAPLETON CASTLE
Probably founded some time after 1144 by the lords of Richard's Castle once they had lost control of Presteigne Castle, it stayed in their hands until it passed by marriage to the Cornewalls at the beginning of the 14th century. The castle then consisted of a motte on the high southern end of the knoll, with a ditch cut along the western and eastern sides; a bailey was constructed to the north. The castle buildings on the motte had largely been replaced by a fortified manor house by the time of the Civil War, and this was slighted by the local Royalist commander, Sir Michael Woodhouse, in 1645. In 1706 it passed into the hands of the Harley family, and it had been abandoned by the end of the 1800s.

boundary on your left and so out through a gate and the drive to a house and onto a road.

5 Turn left on the road, and fork right at the junction soon reached. Keep following this into Stapleton, and shortly after the road has made a right-hand bend and where it then makes a bend to the left, keep ahead on a bridleway that enters a field. Keep to the right-hand edge of the field and at its end the bridleway becomes hedged on each side. Keep following this bridleway till it meets another road.

6 Turn left on this road and follow it past a couple of lanes off to the right, the second signposted for Middlemoor Barn. Soon after this lane, and just past a telegraph pole, you'll reach a wide opening through the hedge on your right. The circular route bears right here, but you may wish to carry on to Bryan's Ground a few hundred yards further on on the right, before returning this way. (If you go to Bryan's Ground, you first pass, on the right, Bryan's Ground Cottage and then Little Bryan's Ground. The entrance to Bryan's Ground comes next, just past a Royal Mail letterbox.)

> **BRYAN'S GROUND**
> This comprises a 3-acre Arts and Crafts style garden consisting of various 'rooms' of different themes, and a 5-acre arboretum with specimen trees and shrubs. In 2016 it was open to the public on Sunday and Monday afternoons between mid April and mid August, but best to check for current opening times on 01544 260001 or at http://www.bryansground.co.uk.

7 Facing the opening in the hedge, you want to turn half right to cross a corner of the field, heading back to the lane that serves Middlemoor Barn, aiming for a point midway between a barn and a black and white timber-framed house. When you reach the hedge you'll find a stile to cross. Cross the lane and another stile on its far side to enter another field. Follow the hedge on your left to another stile and then keep following the field boundary on your left. This will lead you to a little wooden gate just past a house which you go through to come out onto a lane.

Turn right on the lane, and almost immediately left down a gravelled track. At its end, go through the field gate on the right. Follow the hedge on the right to a gate at the far end of the field. Go through this, cross the driveway to a kissing gate, and then follow the path above the Lugg till you reach a road which you should recognize.

8 Turn left on the road and walk back to the church. Keep walking up Broad Street, passing the Judge's Lodgings on the left, and at the Victorian Brick Assembly Rooms and Library turn right into the High Street. Follow this along, passing the Radnorshire Arms and then a garage on your left.

Immediately past the garage turn left, then cross the main road, and walk on up the minor road on its far side.

BROAD STREET

Houses to look out for walking up Broad Street include, first, on the left, Tan House. This has a rebuilt hall with a box-framed cross wing. It has been tree-ring dated to 1436. Next, also on the left, is Oak Villas, a cruck-framed hall house with jettied wings. Then, on the right, is Well House where a medieval cross wing of three bays survives, with a jettied side over a passage. Back on the left is Fold Farm, which comprises a hall and cross wing. On the right comes the Old Bridge of the 16th century, with a jettied front of three bays to the street, followed by No.9 and The White House. No. 9 has a box-framed cross wing of two chambers, and there are signs of a cruck-framed hall at the White House. Further on, on the left-hand side comes Hafod, which retains fragments of a storeyed box-framed cross wing and side jetty, and the Duke's Arms, a 16th-century storeyed house with a central passage and jettied front to the street.

PRESTEIGNE

A probable Saxon settlement preceded the 'vill' recorded in the second quarter of the 12th century, between which times it had suffered at the hands of Gruffydd ap Llywelyn in 1052. A weekly market and annual fair was granted sometime between 1230 and 1250, probably as a result of Mortimer desire to encourage the settlement to grow, and from this time the town had a period of prosperity. The regular pattern of streets to the south-west of the church suggest a planned settlement, with the High Street as the main axis; some of the lanes that run parallel to Broad Street could be part of the original medieval street pattern. Broad Street was probably the site of the medieval market.

Perhaps commencing with the arrival of the Black Death in the mid 1300s followed by widespread depredations during the Glyndwr uprising five decades later, the town fell into decline. It did not recover until it benefited from the patronage of Richard Martin, a native of the town and bishop of St Davids. Presteigne received a charter in 1482 and benefited from the woollen industry in the following years.

The role of county town for the shire of Radnorshire, created under the Acts of Union of England and Wales in the 1530s and 1540s, was initially shared between Rhayader and New Radnor. However, when the judge visited Rhayader to preside at the first Great Sessions (to be held twice yearly in each county and covering cases of major felony and misdemeanour), he was attacked and killed, and Presteigne replaced Rhayader as the venue for the Great Sessions and became recognised as the county town after 1660. It was in Presteigne that the county assizes, as they became known, were then held until the 20th century. Meanwhile the growth of Llandrindod Wells meant that it would become the seat of local government for the county council in 1888 though Presteigne remained the county town. It was only with the reorganization of local government in 1974 and the abolition of Radnorshire and the formation of Powys as the unit of local government, that it lost this status, Llandrindod Wells then becoming the county town of Powys. Assizes continued to be held at Presteigne till 1970. The slightly idiosyncratic Judge's Lodgings Museum is well worth a visit (see p.99).

A fire in 1681 destroyed between 50 and 70 houses to the immediate north of the church and to its west and south-west, meaning that the town's earliest houses stand in Broad Street (see p.97) and Hereford Street, together with the Radnorshire Arms. The fortunes of the town then depended upon its status as the county town and the wellbeing or otherwise of the local agricultural industry, rising in times of farming prosperity such as the 1850s and 1860s (when the Market Hall and Assembly rooms were built), and falling in times of agricultural depression. Thus in 1901 the town's population was 28% lower than it had been in 1871. A short-lived boom in forestry brought about by the need for timber in the trenches during the First World War and a vibrant cattle market in the 1920s brought temporary revived prosperity until the years of the Great Depression. Two firms that began operation in Presteigne during the Second World War as part of the government's dispersal programme to counter German bombing brought a degree of prosperity back to the town after that war. The town's population has only really grown again, however, since the 1970s with new housing, new businesses and a concentration of secondary education in eastern Radnorshire at the John Beddoes School.

JUDGE'S LODGINGS

The Shire Hall that stood at the junction of Broad Street and the High Street and which was used for the hearings of the Great Sessions was in need of replacement by the 1820s, whilst the gaol was in such a state of disrepair that walls needed propping up and escapes were commonplace. A new gaol was built and the site of the old gaol in Broad Street used to build a new Shire Hall with lodgings for the judge, so replacing the old lodgings at the same time. The new building was completed in 1829.

With the last assizes being held in the building in 1970, a new use needed to be found for it, otherwise decay and demolition beckoned. Fortunately the building was still in reasonable condition, whilst the attics were found to be full of furniture, glassware, silverware and portraits. It was decided to recreate the building in its mid Victorian heyday, to the extent of replacing the electric lights with oil lamps, candles and gas lighting. Replica wallpapers were used and carpets made to Victorian patterns. Audio tours were created in which those who used or worked in the building tell their story. With the help of these, you can visit the judge's living quarters, the servants' work areas and the cells that held the prisoners before trial. From this dismal dungeon you can enter the court as if you were one of those prisoners. Once in the court, you can hear a dramatisation of the 1860s trial of William Morgan, accused of stealing ducks from Llanshay Farm in Knighton. There is also a museum about wider Presteigne.

THE RADNORSHIRE ARMS

Originally called the Cross House, the Radnorshire Arms was built in the late 1500s and became the country retreat of Sir Charles Hatton, a favourite of Queen Elizabeth I who became Lord Chancellor. In 1616 (the date recorded in the front porch) it was bought by John Bradshaw, one of Presteigne's most prosperous merchants, who enlarged it. It became an inn in 1792, quickly becoming one of the town's main coaching inns (another was the Duke's Arms in Broad Street) and also a venue for society dinners and gatherings. Further enlargements and modernisations have kept its 'black and white' character, and revealed a priest's hole off what is now the residents' lounge. The priest's hole, it is told, held a diary, since lost, that recorded the life of a priest who had hidden there for two years.

PRESTEIGNE CASTLE

The first castle might have been begun by the lords of Richard's Castle even before the Norman Conquest, for Osbern fitz Richard held the land in at least the latter part of Edward the Confessor's reign. Certainly by the time of the Domesday Survey, two men-at-arms are recorded. Whilst the survey records that there was land enough for 20 ploughs, it was still recorded as waste, having not recovered from the events of 1055 when Hereford was sacked and much of the area literally laid waste.

Some time around the mid 1100s, Presteigne Castle passed into the hands of Roger Port of Kington, and the descendants of Osbern fitz Richard built a new castle at Stapleton. The Ports put the de Fraxino family in charge of the castle. When the Ports were banished in 1172 for rebellion, their barony seems to have been managed as part of the responsibilities of the Sheriff of Herefordshire. In 1203 William de Braose bought the barony from King John and when he rebelled against the king, de Fraxino seems to have created his own little barony which he held direct from John. When the de Braoses returned to royal favour under the new king, Henry III, in 1218, de Fraxino's small barony was reincorporated into that of the de Braoses. The Mortimers subsequently acquired the barony by marriage, with the de Fraxinos still in possession of the castle. The Mortimers probably strengthened the defences, but the castle never seems to have been rebuilt in stone, and probably comprised a wooden tower surrounded by an earth bank topped by a palisade.

The castle was destroyed by Llywelyn ap Gruffudd in 1262, and by 1337 was simply 'a plot of land called Castle Ditch'. The site passed into the hands of the Harley family who landscaped the area with flower beds, a promenade and a bowling green. In 1805 the land was presented to the town.

9 Soon you will come to a gate in a stone wall on your right. Go through this onto The Warden, the site of Presteigne's castle. Once you've had a look round, head down the hillside past the picnic tables into a small field and cross down to the far corner of this and onto the main road. Cross this, then turn almost immediately right into Wilson Terrace, which you cross to join a footpath on a wide grassy track.

Walk ahead down this, following it to the far end, and pass through a small gate and down some steps to join another path, on which you turn right. Within a few yards you have an option to turn left and head down yet more steps to make a boardwalk tour of the Withybeds Nature Reserve. The circular walk continues along the path, which soon joins a lane. Keep ahead at the various junctions, then bear slightly left down Church Street when you reach it. This will return you to the church.

Walk 15
New Radnor

8.75 miles largely on tracks and quiet roads with some footpaths. One track can become quite waterlogged in winter and it's advisable to wear Wellington boots. There is one stile. The one ascent is quite gentle, and the descent only slightly steeper. There are good views as you circle the flanks of Radnor Forest. The walk gives you a good chance to explore a prehistoric landscape.

Park in New Radnor.

❶ With your back to the Radnor Arms pub (closed at the time of writing), turn right and walk down the road to reach the memorial to George Cornewall Lewis.

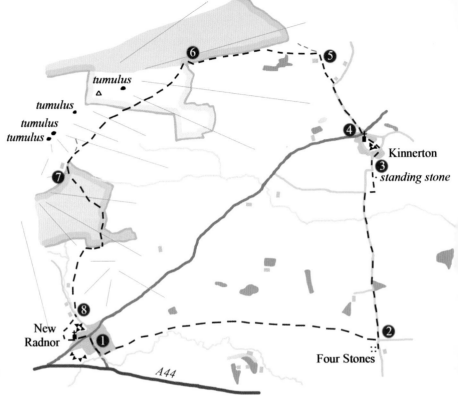

Cross the road on the far side of the memorial and then take School Lane off to the left, just this side of the Summergill brook, and walk along it past the school. The road will lose its tarmacked surface and become first a stoned track then field edge trackway, with the line of the original below you left, before once more becoming a

trackway. At some points the track becomes quite water-logged and you may need to pick your way along the banks at the foot of the hedgerows on either side, but in due course it once again gains a stoned surface. Ignore all the footpath and bridleway signs off to the left, and just keep ahead on the track till you reach a tarmacked lane.

102

NEW RADNOR

The town owed its origins to the Norman castle (for which see p.109). A settlement is likely to have been in existence by 1188, when Archbishop Baldwin came to 'Radnor' to start his preaching tour raising enthusiasm and volunteers for the First Crusade, though in whose hands the town then lay is open to question (see box on the castle). The constant warfare and sieges of the castle abated after the 1260s with further murage grants in 1280, 1283 and 1290, and the town began to flourish in the 1300s. The town walls comprised a bank up to 2.7m high and a ditch 1m deep, with a second, flatter, bank on the outer side. In 1301 the town had 97 burgesses and just three years later 189 burgesses. A comparatively prosperous settlement is also indicated by the rents and tolls collected in 1360, despite the occurrence in the meantime of the Black Death.

In 1536 with the Union of England and Wales, New Radnor and Rhayader were to share the duties of the shire town for the newly created Radnorshire, duties which gradually passed to Presteigne and then Llandrindod Wells (see p.98). In 1562 it gained borough status and was governed by 25 'capital burgesses' and soon had four annual fairs. By 1731 the town was down to seven burgesses. Its Parliamentary constituency was done away with in 1880 and the borough six years later.

GEORGE CORNEWALL LEWIS MEMORIAL

First elected to parliament as a Liberal MP for a Herefordshire seat in 1847, on the death of his father he fought a by-election for the Radnorshire Boroughs seat in 1855, and remained its MP until he died in 1863. At times he was Home Secretary, Chancellor of the Exchequer and Minister for War. His interests, however, seem to have lain more in history and languages: he wrote many articles and books, notably on the history of the Romans, and spoke several modern and ancient European languages. His home was at nearby Harpton Court.

The memorial was designed by John Gibbs of Oxford, chosen from 59 designs that were submitted. Described as 'somewhat in the style of an Eleanor Cross', it includes a medallion portrait of Lewis and four 6 feet tall allegorical figures representing Justice, Truth, Oratory and Literature, the coats of arms of England, Ireland, Scotland and Wales, and four griffins holding the arms of the Lewis family.

THE FOUR STONES AND THE WALTON BASIN

The Walton basin, the bed of a former glacial lake, is known for its large agglomeration of prehistoric sites, most of which are only visible as cropmarks, with the exception of the Four Stones, some barrows and the occasional standing stone. But it is worth standing at the Four Stones and trying to take in the prehistoric landscape, for one of two cursuses (earthwork enclosures comprising parallel banks and sometimes standing stones or upright timbers) ran just 20m to the south of the stones.

First, have a look around the horizon and you'll see hills on all sides, for the main entrances and exits to the basin are hidden behind shoulders of hills. This seems to have made the area attractive as a centre for religious or ritual purposes. Of the two cursuses, the largest lies near the village of Walton, indeed partly under it. It ran south-west to north-east for 680m and has well spaced parallel ditches. A barrow lies close to its south-western end, and it was overlain by several later enclosures. The other cursus (that which runs just to the south of the Four Stones) ran on a roughly similar alignment for 465m, and was defined by roughly parallel ditches c.70m apart at either end, but narrowing to 60m apart in the middle. Two substantial barrows lie close to it, whilst 20m from its north-eastern end (and about 500m east of the Four Stones) lies part of the circumference of what is called the Hindwell pallisaded enclosure.

This feature encloses 35ha and is the largest such enclosure yet found in Britain, and indeed is the second largest in Europe, the largest being in Germany. Excavation has revealed that the perimeter is marked by a series of post pits each with a ramp (down which the post could be slid before being raised into an upright position). Remains of carbonised oak were found in the pits, dated to between 2900 and 2460BC, indicating the pits indeed held wooden posts, though it is unknown if these were free standing or had a lintel at the top to form a wooden circle akin in style to Stonehenge. In any event, the posts would appear to have been 0.8m in diameter and, assuming one third of the post was below ground, stood some 6m above ground. With the posts being spaced every 5m and with a circumference of 2.35km (just under 1.5 miles), over 1,400 posts would have been needed. So, look east and imagine such a henge. Surveys have revealed no structures within the henge, but several large pits and two barrows. It was almost certainly used for religious or ritual purposes.

As for the Four Stones, they stand between 0.9m and 1.55m high, and probably only ever numbered four in total. Probably later than the henge and dating to the Bronze Age, they have gathered a degree of folklore to themselves. To some they mark the graves of four kings killed in a nearby battle, whilst in 1925 Alfred Watkins wrote: 'If you stamp on the ground between them it sounds hollow. Fifty years ago, I was told at the Crown [inn] at Walton, "they do say how when the Four Stones hear the sound of Old Radnor bells they go down to Hindwell pool to drink".'

❷ Turn right on this lane and in a few yards you will see the Four Stones in a field on your right. Having had a look (and read about the prehistoric landscape and henges on the opposite page), turn back up the lane and continue on it past the end of the track which you just walked down.

Keep on the lane till you all but reach the second tarmacked lane off to the left. Just a handful of yards before you would reach this lane, go through the gate into a field on your right and follow the field boundary on your left. About 30 yards before you would reach the end of this field, cross the stile on your left into another field, the path then carrying on alongside a hedge on your right. Near the place where the hedge makes a small kink, you want to keep an eye out through the hedge for a standing stone, slightly smaller than one of the Four Stones, that stands towards the far side of the next field. Keep following the hedge up to a gateway and back out onto the road you were recently on.

❸ Turn right on the road, then almost immediately right again, to pass Kinnerton Court on your left. Immediately past this, take the track off to the left and this leads you past the motte of Kinnerton Castle on your left and then out onto a road near the church. Turn left to visit the church, then carry on through the churchyard and so out onto a road.

KINNERTON

The name is derived from 'Cyneheard's farm' or 'settlement' and as such is one of a number of Saxon place-names to the west of Offa's Dyke in the Walton basin. There are remains of some house platforms to the east of the present village, suggesting it was once somewhat larger. Kinnerton Court is of early to mid 18th-century date.

Kinnerton motte still retains its ditch, and a bailey probably lay to the south. The site is naturally wet, and a pond to the immediate north-west of the motte is now a feature of the grounds in which it stands. It is overlooked by higher ground to the north-west, though stands at the end of a small ridge, like many other castles in the area.

Little is known of the castle, though on 31 May 1252, Henry III issued a royal writ confirming that it belonged to Margeria, the daughter of Isolda. On Isolda's death, Roger (III) Mortimer, as Lord of Radnor, had granted the castle to William fitz Elye and others. The royal

writ suggests that Radnor was then seen as part of Herefordshire and not as an independent Marcher lordship.

St Mary's Church was built as a chapel of ease for parishioners in this part of New Radnor parish, and rebuilt in 1884-5. A bank that runs to the west of the church formerly separated the churchyard from a house and its grounds, the land being included in the churchyard during the 19th century, at a time when a graveyard was commenced.

4 Turn left on the road, then almost immediately right, to leave the village hall on your left. Keep on this road and follow it uphill and then round a bend to the right. At this point, just before you reach a white-painted cottage on your left, go through the gate on the left onto a grassy track which is signed as a bridleway. Follow this uphill and it will lead you via a gate into a field. Keep to the right-hand field edge and this will lead you, via another gate, onto a tarmacked lane, to the right of a new house.

5 Turn left on the lane, and then almost immediately left again onto a stoned track. This will lead you alongside the edge of a small wood. When the track turns left to enter a field, keep on following the line of the old sunken way ahead up to the edge of the forestry plantation. Here the sunken way bends left to follow the edge of the plantation, and, keeping following it, you pass through two gates into successive fields. In the top right-hand corner of the second field, by which point you have passed the peak of Stanlow Tump on your left, you pass through a small gate into the woodland itself.

6 After a few yards you reach a stoned forestry track on which you turn left, and then bear left at the fork reached in a further few yards and then pass back out onto the hillside via another gate. Now follow the track you find yourself on that curves away from the forestry and bends gently right. This will lead you along the hillside above steep and deep heads of valleys to your left. Just this side of the top of the ridge on your right are a number of tumuli, not always easy to spot but due to how they are sited you might discern them against the skyline.

As you approach a large barn in a shoulder in the hills, with the prominent hill called the Whimble behind it, another bridleway will join you from the right, by the corner of a small stunted copse. At this point your path technically passes through a gate below the gravelled track and then follows the gravelled track on a parallel grassy track which rejoins the stoned track near the barn.

7 Just past the far end of the barn keep a sharp eye out for and take a small footpath (hopefully still marked by a post) which heads off downhill to the left. Follow this down to meet another stoned forestry track. Turn right on this and after just a few yards, left again down a small path. This will lead you out in due course onto another stoned forestry track. Turn right on this and at the bend soon reached, take the track off to the left and then, when the track splits after just a few yards, the right-hand path; there should be another marker post here. Follow this path downhill and when it comes to the edge of the wood in front of a fence, turn right and follow the fence along to a gate. Once through the gate, keep to the path as it slants downhill to meet a tarmacked lane.

8 Turn left on the lane, pass some tumble-down buildings on the right, then take the footpath off to the right just before the road bends to the left. This path will lead you up and then around and down past the earthen-covered remains of Radnor Castle, then round the lip of a small quarry to a field gate. As you approach this, keep an eye out for the earthen bank ahead of you that marks the line of the old town walls, as seen in the photo on the left. Go through this gate and then follow the old stone wall and bank on your left to enter the churchyard by a small gate.

NEW RADNOR CASTLE

New Radnor Castle has probably seen more sieges than most castles in the land. The first, earthwork, castle might have been built by Philip de Braose in the 1090s. The castle may have suffered its first siege in 1182 and been taken by Rhys ap Gruffydd of Deheubarth, but if so it had been retaken by the de Braoses in 1195, for it was captured (possibly for the second time) by Rhys the following year. However, it must have again been back in de Braose hands by 1208 when King John took control of the castle and exiled its lord William de Braose. However, forces loyal to de Braose took it in 1215, only for John to capture and partially destroy it the following year. It was rebuilt by Reginald de Braose just a few years later, but captured and destroyed again in 1231, this time by Llywelyn ab Iorwerth. It was rebuilt in 1233-35, this time by Richard, Earl of Cornwall, brother to Henry III who was campaigning against the Welsh, and obtained a murage grant in 1257. Nevertheless, in 1264 it was captured and destroyed yet again, this time by Llywelyn ap Gruffudd, when in alliance with Simon de Montfort. It was subsequently rebuilt by the Mortimers.

The castle was put into a state of defence during the wars with Owain Glyndwr with command of the garrison held by Sir John Greyndour, a Gloucestershire knight. A tale tells of a devastating raid made into eastern Radnorshire in 1401 by Glyndwr's forces which saw the slaughtering of the castle garrison. When the church was rebuilt in 1845 a mass grave was found in one spot in the churchyard and a pit containing 'a corresponding number' of skulls in another, and folklore has ascribed these remains to be of the castle garrison slaughtered in 1401, though there is no proof of the raid nor dating of the skeletons. Whatever the truth, the castle itself cannot have been too badly damaged in any such raid, for by June 1403 the garrison amounted to more than 70 men, at a time when Brecon was under siege, and in 1405 had grown to 180 men, of whom 150 were archers. By now the English tactic had developed into a number of castle garrisons acting in consort, with fast-moving flying columns being co-ordinated to attack Welsh forces discovered to be in the area.

Once the Glyndwr threat was thwarted, the castle was probably abandoned. Leland, c.1538, noted that the 'towne was defacyd in Henry the Fowthe dayes by Owen Glindour' and that 'the castle is in ruine' whilst the town was 'metley [mostly] well wallyd, and in the walle appere the ruines of iiii gates'. He also noted that many of the houses were thatched. Despite Leland's comments, the castle was reputedly garrisoned by the Royalists during the Civil War and successfully besieged by Parliamentary forces.

The castle motte was sculpted from a natural hill around the top of which a wall or ringwork was built with a bailey to the north-west. A drawing made by John Speed in 1610 shows the walls still standing to the height of the battlements, though no buildings remained apart from the gate tower on the north-west, at the entry from the bailey. The walls appear to have had a number of D-shaped towers, and parts were still standing in 1815. Parts of the bailey appear to have been cultivated once the castle had fallen out of use, for there are traces of ridges and furrows. Excavations in 1864 revealed foundations, arched doorways and windows and a well in the castle's dungeon.

Go through the churchyard to the road, visiting the church if you wish. Once you reach the road, you might want to turn right to have a look at the old Oak Inn (see photo, left) just along on the right-hand side of the road, but to return to the Radnor Arms, turn left and then right at the road junction ahead.

OLD HOUSES

8 Church Street (Swan House) is a truncated 15th-century cruck-built house (two crucks remain) refaced in stone in the 19th century. It was originally built as a meeting place and had a thatched roof. It had become an inn by the 1830s and probably remained one till just after the First World War. Opposite is what used to be the Oak Inn in the 16th century.

1 and 2 High Street were formerly part of the Cross Inn built in the 17th century; 11 High Street was originally a timber-framed house of the 16th or 17th century, but partially rebuilt and refaced in stone.

New Radnor has been described as one of the best examples in Wales of a shrunken medieval planted town, and a walk around its streets shows the laid-out pattern, with house platforms and earthwork boundaries of disappeared houses, and the various remnants of the town defences.

CHURCH OF ST MARY

The church is thought to have been founded in the 12th or 13th century as an element of the new borough; certainly a document of 1291 refers to it as Ecclesia de Radenore Nova. A new church is thought to have been erected at the expense of William and Flory Bachefeld in the 14th century close to the site of the earlier church. Speed's map of the early 17th century shows a church with a west tower, probably with a corner turret, a large nave with a south porch and a smaller chancel, but it is not known how accurate a picture this was. By 1818 a south aisle had been added, and 'a timber frame' was noted as dividing the chancel from the nave. This screen was partially sketched by John Parker prior to the church's demolition in preparation for the current building constructed in 1843-45, a church described as having 'no pretence of architectural consideration'. The south transept might have been added slightly later, paid for by the Lewis family of Downton House.

Whatever one may think of the church's architectural merits, it does have some features of interest. The entrance is through the tower, where stairs lead up to the ringing chamber. Inside the church itself, parts of the old screen have been used in the communion rails, while two worn effigies recovered from the churchyard are currently (2016) on display in the south transept, having been thought to have previously lain outside the church (due to their weathered nature) then lain in darkened obscurity on the floor of the tower. The figure with the unusual round shield was once thought to be of Philip de Braose, a crusader, but is now thought to be Einion o'r Porth, a descendant of Elystan Glodrydd (for whom see page 12) and the other, his wife Maud de Mortimer.

On the south side of the churchyard there is a drop into the neighbouring field, while on the west there is an earth and rubble bank displaying a drystone wall in places – the remnants of the town defences.

Walk 16
Llanvihangel

7 miles, largely on tracks with some paths and a short section of A road (which has a pavement for part and wide verge for the rest). There are a couple of stiles, one of which is followed by a very steep bank to clamber up, which can also be clad in nettles and brambles; a walking stick could be useful to quell the vegetation. If you're walking with a dog, keep it on a lead when passing through the SSSI, which is being restored as a breeding ground for grouse. The walk takes in an interesting range of upland history, from the prehistoric to more recent farming, and even film-making. Two pubs lie near the end of the walk, or can be returned to once you've completed the whole circuit.

Park at Llynheilyn.

❶ Take the track to the right of the lake and cross the ford at the edge of the parking area. Go through the field gate and then immediately take the

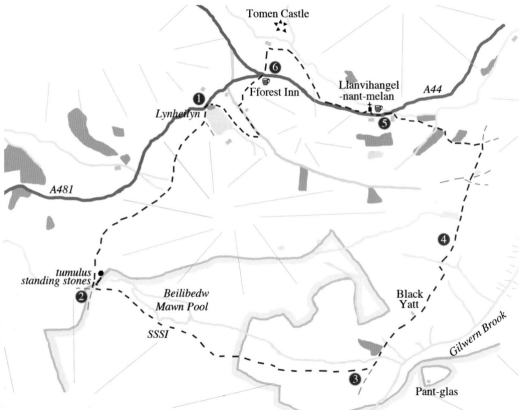

LLYNHEILYN

If the lake has a mournful air, that may be because it is haunted, or so some say. Silver John was a bone setter and wore a coat sewn with many silver buttons, either given him by grateful people whose bones he had set, or gifts of money he had had turned into buttons as a way of keeping his wealth close. Perhaps unsurprisingly, as the coat became ever more valuable, the thought of stealing it grew in the minds of some. Thus it was that one night, some time between c.1770 and 1780, he failed to return to his home in the Harley valley on the southern slopes of Radnor Forest. A search was mounted, but to no avail. A few months later a Candlemas Fair was held on the lake, during which the daughter of the landlord of the nearby Fforest Inn tripped and fell flat on the ice, to find herself staring at the remains of Silver John.

track off to the right. Through a second gate, take the left hand of the two tracks and follow it along the fenceline on your left. The track initially slants uphill and then contours round the hillside. In due course pass through a third gateway and follow the fence now on your right-hand side.

The next gateway you reach is near the crest of the ridge and once through it you'll find yourself approaching a wide upland valley that slopes gently downhill to your left. Ahead of you you'll see a prominent tumulus near the valley bottom, and it is this you head towards, keeping it just to your left. Beyond this you'll come to a line of very small standing stones known as Bryn y Maen.

2 Immediately past the standing stones is a meeting way of several tracks. Cross one track, and then take the one to the left that follows the wide valley downhill. Go through a gate and keep going downhill towards the group of Scots

BRYN Y MAEN

A line of five standing stones, two of which are now recumbent, stand up to 0.8m high in a line 16.5m in length. Thirteen Bronze Age round barrows, erected at a probably similar date to the standing stones, have now been identified in the nearby hills, one of them close to the line of standing stones. Only one of these barrows, on Llanfihangel Hill just to the east of this walk, has been dug into haphazardly in the past. As a result, some scattered stony material lies around what is presumed to have been a central cist (a small stone-lined grave) that may have held an urn containing ashes. (For more on tumuli see pages 139 and 146.)

pines at the bottom. Here there's a gate into an SSSI located around Beilibedw Mawn Pool where red grouse breed. (The pool is to your left but not always immediately visible because of all the reeds.) Keep on the track past the Mawn Pool; it passes just to the right of the top of a small rise in the valley and then drops down to a gate out of the SSSI. Keep on the track through the valley, heading towards a small group of trees. Go through a gate under a sycamore and keep straight on. Fifty yards or so beyond the gate, you'll come to a fork of two tracks. Take the left-hand fork, which follows a field boundary on your left through an area marked by the remnants of old field divisions.

LLUESTS

In the valleys in the hills on this walk, and on other walks, you might at times (depending upon the extent of bracken cover and the angle of any sunlight) be able to make out the now earth- and turf-covered embankments marking the remains of lluests, upland farmsteads. Some may relate to attempts to gain a living from the hills down the centuries, but most were constructed during the 17th and 18th centuries, when adjacent landowners sought to establish claims to the open hillsides, and were used by those employed to guard and milk cattle and for processing cheese and butter. They were thus often sited near fresh running streams which would provide a source of clean water, whilst also being slightly sheltered in the valleys. Their siting seems to have been regulated by court leets with lawful occupation granted between 15 May and 15 August. In due course some were permanently occupied as landowners sought to extend their 'rights' and developed them into farmsteads, shallow pools being constructed to retain water over the summer months to supplement the naturally occurring peat or mawn pools, and often traces of ridge and furrow ploughing being visible when not covered by heather or bracken.

One of the most prominent groups of these farmsteads is on this walk beyond the Site of Special Scientific Interest. The footprints of at least three buildings, various enclosures and a dam across the Gilwern brook can be seen.

The farmsteads were generally abandoned during the 1800s.

BLACK YATT AND PANT GLAS

These were two of the few lluests still inhabited at the time of the 1830s tithe surveys. Pant Glas is still occupied, but Black Yatt was blown up in the 1960s during the making of the film *It Happened Here*, directed, written and produced by teenagers Kevin Brownlow and Andrew Mollo (though the years it took to make the film saw them enter their twenties). It is set in 1944, four years after an imagined successful German invasion of Britain, and in the story partisans try to overthrow the regime. It caused much controversy due to its depiction of Britons collaborating with occupying German forces.

③ This track leads you to the right of a small piece of woodland where you meet another track. Turn left on this, ford the stream and walk up the right-hand edge of the woodland, following the track over another ford and gently uphill and past the remains of Black Yatt. Once through the next gateway you come into an area of improved grassland. Once you've crossed another ford near the top of a prominent gully which leads down into Cwm-y-bont, the area on your right is noted for several pillow mounds and house platforms, not that it is easy to see any of them from the path.

④ Go through a gate and keep following the track and it will lead all of a sudden to a large pool near the crest of the hill. Keep to the immediate right of the pool, and once through two gates and in the field beyond, turn half left in relation to the fenceline on your right and walk across the field to a gate, which you will see as you cross the field. (Walk in a line slightly to the left of the mast on the horizon.) Go through this gate and drop downhill on a track to a meeting of tracks just to the left of a small pool. Cross two tracks and go through the gate straight ahead. The path now follows the fenceline on your right and drops down to a crossroads of paths, where you turn

CHURCH OF ST MICHAEL, LLANFIHANGEL NANT MELAN

W.H. Howse, one of Radnorshire's historians, recorded a tradition that the church is 'said to have been placed within the ring of a stone circle; an ancient stone will be noticed embedded in the hollow trunk of one of the yews', echoing the thought that some churches were purposefully built on the site of pagan shrines so as to absorb allegiance to the former religion. However, only one stone has ever been found, making the claim for it to be part of a circle difficult to substantiate, though there are reports of there having been a second stone in the churchyard and a third one in the car park of the Red Lion. The church certainly seems to sit within the boundary of a former enclosure of some description.

The church belonged to the de Braose family, who gave it in the later 12th century to the Knights Hospitaller. In 1818 it was described as 'a very low and mean edifice, constructed with the perishable stone of the country, and externally whitewashed. Its internal appearance contains nothing worthy of notice.' In 1846 it was completely rebuilt in the Norman style, possibly consciously modelled on Kilpeck Church in Herefordshire, by Thomas Nicholson, the then diocesan architect.

The church sits on a level platform some 2m high on the north where it incorporates the river terrace edge, though the platform's other edges are artificial. Five mature yews (a sixth has been cut down) ring the south side of the church. One suggestion is that the mound was once topped by a yew venerable in age even to prehistoric man, and that a ring of offshoots was formed by the rooting of branches from this parent tree, which subsequently died.

To the west of the churchyard, now covered by a small plantation, is a linear bank heading across the valley floor. This could be a valley screen bank, a smaller version of, for example, the Rowe Ditch (and bank) which crosses the Arrow valley to the west of Pembridge in Herefordshire, and thus perhaps be Saxon in origin. If so, it would predate the earthworks associated with a medieval mill which comprise a leat, a pond and a building platform. Other earthworks and platforms might relate to buildings associated with the mill or to dwellings, and some such features are believed to have been lost to recent landscaping.

Great House, opposite the church, retains the remnants of a 15th-century open hall house.

left on the well defined track. This will lead down the hillside, just above some woodland and into the farmyard at Lower House farm. Once past the first series of barns bear right to reach the main road.

5 Turn left on the main road and you'll soon come to the Red Lion on your right, and then Llanvihangel church, built in 1846.

RED LION
This began life as a drovers' inn, and is where Silver John (see page 114) is supposed to have conducted much of his business.

Keep on the right-hand side of the main road on a wide verge till you reach a track off to the right which you take. (It's just past the speed deregulation sign on the road.) Follow this track

along, passing a new house on your left and keeping an eye out for Tomen Castle, a prominent Norman motte off to your right. (It may not be possible to see it from here if you're walking when there's a lot of foliage on the trees.) When you reach some barns on the right of the track, turn left across the field, aiming for the middle of the white painted Fforest Inn that stands on the main road. As you cross the field, do turn round to look at Tomen Castle; you can see it from here whatever time of year it is. At the bottom of the bank on the far side of the field you'll reach a stile, which you cross, then clamber up the bank. Note that although this is a mercifully short climb, it's quite steep and the path is sometimes overgrown and nettly.

TOMEN CASTLE

In a document of 1231 that confirms a previous grant, William de Braose and Meurig ab Ade (possibly one and the same as Meurig ab Ieuaf) granted the church of Nant Melan to St Davids. This suggests that the nearby Tomen Castle would have been built by the de Braoses but possibly held by Welsh allies, a branch of the princely family of Maelienydd. However, it is possibly the site of a Welsh castle built by one of the sons of Einion Clud, a descendant of Elystan Glodrydd (see page 12) who ruled the cantref of Elfael.

It is possible (depending upon problems of identification) that Meurig's father had led troops in the armies of Henry II in his wars on the Continent, but Meurig himself had been fined by King John, who had led a short victorious campaign against Llywelyn ab Iorwerth in 1211. With John's complicated relationship with the de Braoses, at one time close allies then the bitterest of enemies, the allegiance of many Welsh families in the Marches must have been tested time and again. Certainly John was at war with the Welsh again in 1212, when some of the Marchers and King John took to hanging any hostages they had held as good security of their brethren. John was to hang Meurig Barach, believed to be the last lord of Tomen Castle, at Bridgnorth, and it is possible that the castle was destroyed in this period of warfare.

FFOREST INN

This was once a drovers' inn, which had ground for stock at the rear, and then it became a coaching inn. It was the subject of a novel written in 1946, appropriately called *Forest Inn*, by H.L.V. Fletcher, set in the period after Waterloo. Whilst the story revolves around the inn and the novel describes the exterior fairly accurately, the description of the interior is more fanciful.

6 Cross the main road and head between the Fforest Inn and a house to its right, to go through a gate onto a track. Follow this track along the fence on your right to the next field, which you cross keeping just to the right of the trees standing in the field. Here you will reach a stile which you cross to reach a metalled lane. Turn left on this and walk along it for a few hundred yards, passing a cottage on your left and a field gate on your right, till you reach a small gate on your right. Go through this and turn back towards the lake, heading to another small gate at the left-hand end of the fence ahead. Go through this, to then walk along the fence by the lake, passing through a field gate further on. Once past the corner of the lake, the path heads up to the right of a copse to leave through a small gate onto the main road. Turn left on this and walk the few yards back to where you parked.

Walk 17
The Pales

6 miles, on a mixture of tracks, quiet roads and paths. The walk is most easily done when bracken is not at its height of rumbustiousness. The walk does start with an awkward gate to engage with (it is very broken and tied up with all kinds of twine), followed by either a track passing through or around fallen trees amongst bracken, or by making a very steep ascent of the hillside. Once that is accomplished, the walk becomes much easier! There is one other quite long but generally gradual ascent, but no stiles and great views.

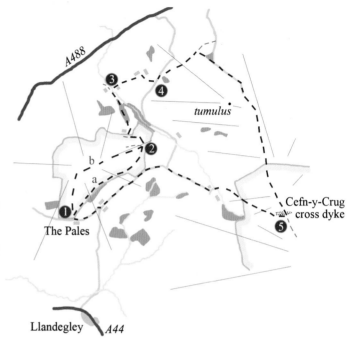

Follow the signs to The Pales from either the A488 just north-east of Penybont, or the A44 at Llandegley. If you're coming from Llandegley, having turned north off the A44, after about a mile you need to turn sharply left and uphill. (It's the first road junction you reach, and is signposted 'The Pales'; it's just before a large complex of farm buildings.) Just past The Pales (the thatched building on the left near the top of the hill), you'll come to a small quarry on the right. Park here. If you're coming from Penybont, you'll find the quarry on your left at the top of the hill; park here. You can choose to visit The Pales at the start or the end of your walk.

THE PALES

The origin of The Pales lies in the acquisition of a quarter-acre burial ground, on a 1,000 year lease, by a group of Quakers, or Friends, as they were not allowed burial on church land. The lease possibly included buildings, for a meeting of Friends in 1683 held somewhere in the parish of Llandegley was broken up by the High Sheriff (it was a time of persecution of Quakers), and certainly by 1716 The Pales included a 'dwelling house with all the houses and outhouses, garden and woods growing at the lower end of the dwelling house' along with a small piece of land that included the burial ground. Its name is thought to have come from the fence or pales which protected the boundary of the graveyard.

Many Radnorshire Quakers were to emigrate to America, especially Pennsylvania, and by the mid 1800s the community based on The Pales was barely functioning. But Quaker evangelism saw the establishment of The Pales Mission in 1867 which sought to extend Quakerism throughout Radnorshire. A school was built, one of the teachers being Yardley Warner, an American who campaigned for the rights of slaves and came to Britain initially to raise money to pay for the education of freed slaves. The Wardens' Cottage was built for him and his wife, Anne. The school had 40 pupils at its height, but closed in 1889, the Mission itself ending two years later. The community once again dwindled. Then, in the 1970s, the cottage was renovated, wardens were re-appointed, the meeting house was re-thatched and the graveyard was restored.

It now serves as a place for Quaker meetings and worship, as well as a place of quietness for all.

An attempt was made to work a lead mine in the area.

❶ The walk itself starts by heading up along the fence along the end of the quarry closest to The Pales and heading onto open hillside through a rickety tumbledown gate. You then have a choice of routes:

a) There is a 'bridleway' (more a series of sheep tracks) which shadows the fenceline along the bottom of the hill on your right. You will pass an old wood where many trees have been blown onto the hillside, partially blocking the path at times. The way can also be semi-obscured by bracken in summer and autumn. In due course the edge of the open hillside boundary will drop away to the right to meet a road, but here you continue on along the hillside and before long you'll see a gravelled track coming up from the road. Turn left along this track at a point of your choosing, and when another track bears left up the hill, keep going straight ahead on the track you're on.

b) Alternatively, from the tumbledown gate you can walk straight up the steep side of the hill to the crest, turn right and walk along the ridge. When you come to patches of bracken, keep a little to the right of the ridge and look for a way through the bracken. Keep an eye open for the tumulus that sits on top of the hill on the other side of the narrow valley. Keep going straight ahead, heading for a group of farm buildings as the hill slopes down, and you will eventually come to a place where two tracks meet. Turn left along the lower of the two tracks.

2 This track is where the two alternative routes meet. Follow the track along, and presently you'll come to fields on your right. Go through the first field gate, just past the first small field and before a building, onto an old track between fields. Follow this down as it swings gently left, passing field gateways on opposite sides of the track, and it will bring you via a wooden gate at its end into a field. Keep to the right of the old sunken way-cum-stream bed through the field and follow it past alders and ash trees. Where the stream on your left makes a turn to the right, cross it and keep straight ahead to the right of a collection of barns and leave the fields by a gate out onto a tarmacked lane.

3 Turn right on the lane and walk past a house and on for several hundred yards to enter a farmyard. Take the track

off to the right just in front of the farmhouse, and follow this uphill, staying with it as it bends slightly left, and walk up to a gate out onto a road.

4 Turn left on the road and after a couple of hundred yards, take the track off to the right (signposted as a byway), which slants up along the hillside. Keep to the right where it forks, and this will swing you round to the

right and past a small wood to join a road. Keep ahead on the road which continues to lead you uphill. The road gives way to a track, on which you stay, keeping a barn to your left. The tumulus you may have seen from a distance at the start of the walk can now be made out on the crest of the hill on your right.

Keep following the track, which stays close to fences to your left, through a number of fields, taking in the sweeping views to your right. In due course you'll pass through a gate onto open hillside and gently descend. When you reach the lowest point on this track, you should be able to make out the line of a shallow cross dyke.

5 On the other side of this dyke, turn right and pick up the path that heads initially gently downhill, with a stream-incised gully to your left. This path become more obvious as you go downhill and leads to a gate off the hillside and a short length of track to another gate out onto a road. Turn right on the road and keep right at the junction immediately reached. At the next junction, reached after about a third of a mile, turn left, then after about half a mile, just past a group of farm buildings, turn right up another lane to return to The Pales.

CEFN Y CRUG CROSS DYKE

There are examples of many dykes crossing valleys in the Marches, not least the Ditch Bank to the west of New Radnor and the longer Rowe Ditch to the west of Pembridge across the border in Herefordshire. These were probably erected in Saxon times to provide some defence, at least against cattle rustlers from Wales who would have struggled to take cattle over ditches and up the banks. Whilst the Rowe Ditch would have been rendered less necessary by the construction of Offa's Dyke, the Ditch Bank lay a few miles west of the Dyke in an area partially populated by Saxons (on the basis of the placenames) who must have felt more vulnerable.

This dyke, however, is not a valley dyke, fairly clearly! It is about 300m long. Sampling of the ground by auger suggests that the ditch was originally c.2.8m wide and up to 0.9m below original ground level. The bank has spread as the result of erosion over time. The fact that the ditch is on the inside curve of the dyke suggests that the dyke was not a defensive feature but possibly a boundary marker for the limit of the medieval hunting grounds of Radnor Forest. This is lent credence by the fact that the dyke 'cuts off' a lobe of high ground that extends from the bulk of the Radnor Forest 'massif'. Indeed, many dykes constructed in what would have been Welsh territory are most likely to have been boundary markers of one sort or another.

Walk 18
Llandegley

7.75 miles on a mixture of footpaths, open hillside, quiet roads and tracks. You can avoid stiles by not doing the short extension of the walk to the site of the sulphurous springs and Trefonen mill, but be warned – there is one extremely awkward gate to cross on the outward journey to the far end of the ridge. The walk back is below upstanding planes of volcanic rock and laminated ashes.

Park near the church.

❶ Leave the churchyard through the metal kissing gate on the far side of the churchyard from the road. Walk down the slope and across the field to a point just to the right of the far left-hand corner, passing through a gate here and then over a bridge into the next field. Cross this field to the far left-hand corner and go through another gate. Walk up the hillside ahead on a wide grassy path, to meet a track on which you turn left and continue through an old quarry and on up the hillside towards a house.

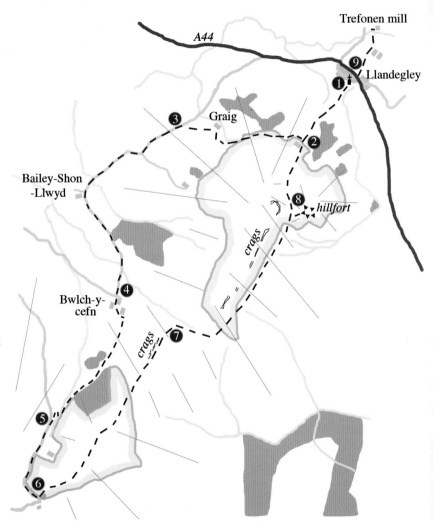

130

CHURCH OF ST TECLA, LLANDEGLEY

St Tecla was a companion of St Paul and died a virgin martyr, but a dedication to such a saint in this part of Wales would be unusual. It is possible that the dedication is therefore to an Irish saint of that name who is known to have visited Cornwall, or more likely that the name refers to some local Celtic saint. A 13th-century manuscript about the life and miracles of St Tecla includes stories of the punishment and repentance of three Radnor robbers, the restoration of a man's sight and one involving two women from 'de uilla Peona', possibly one of the Pyon villages in Herefordshire.

The shape of the churchyard implies an early medieval foundation. There is little obvious sign, however, of any early structure unless it remains in parts of the walls and the south door (which some believe may have come from Cwmhir Abbey when that was rebuilt in 1228). The nave was rebuilt in 1876 along with the chancel, though this might have been an extension to the floor plan of the earlier church. The tower was rebuilt in 1953, following its collapse in 1947.

Just before the restoration of 1876, the screen was described as in poor condition, but still supporting a later gallery reached by a staircase from the chancel. The chancel was separated from the nave by a timber partition. The gallery was done away with when the screen was re-erected as part of the restoration.

2 Just before you reach the house, go through a gateway and immediately turn right on a path that initially follows the boundary of the house now on your left. Keep following the path along the hillside, the path weaving slightly to left and right but essentially following the fenceline on your right. It drops down into a small gully, passes through a gate and over a small stream and continues to follow the fenceline, soon passing by a pair of gates at right angles to each other, to reach another gate across what has now become a track. Go through this gate and follow the track down to meet another track, near which there may be a number of old vehicles and caravans, on which you turn right. Follow this down to a road, passing through the farmyard of Graig farm as you do so.

3 Turn left on the road and follow this along, keeping right at one road junction, and in about two-thirds of a mile you fork left to walk through another farmyard, this time of Bailey-Shon-Llwyd farm, keeping the farmhouse to your right. An assortment of poultry may be wandering about. Keep on the road and it will lead you to a third farm, Bwlch-y-cefn.

4 Here your route crosses over a road, enters the farm-yard to the right of a red brick bungalow, and slants gently uphill, keeping to the left of all the farm buildings except the farmhouse itself, which you stay to the right of. Alongside the farmhouse, the track turns right to then roughly follow the contour of the hill on your left. When the track forks, keep right and downhill to a gate, which you go through to enter a field. Keep on what is

now a faint track which roughly follows the left-hand field boundary, to pass to the left of a block of woodland. Head up the bank on the far side of this woodland so as to keep close to the field boundary on your left, and presently you'll follow the remnants of a stone wall (various tracks and paths lead through the bracken), and head into a tongue of the field between the wall on your left and a slope down to a stream on your right. In the far corner of the field you will come to a rather tumbledown gate which you need to cross. Once over this obstacle, follow the line of the track ahead, which soon drops down to ford the steam (a fairly easy step across). On the far bank, the path dog-legs back up the slope. When you emerge at the top of the bank (having walked about 40 yards from the stream), you want to bear left, aiming to pass close by the first cable-carrying pole, and to the right of the second

to then head towards a gateway near the far right-hand corner of the field that leads into the next field. Go into this next small field and head to its top right-hand corner where you leave it by a gate onto the road.

5 Turn left on the road and follow it along. The road bends left and where it then starts to bend right, you want to aim for the gate on the left into a field just this side of a small copse. (If you reach a small corrugated barn by the side of the road, you're on the wrong side of the copse!)

6 Once in the field, ignore the track off to the left and walk up the rise ahead of you. As you crest this first rise you'll see the line of an old track through the grass, and it's this track you need to join. You'll pass through

another gate and then the track keeps to the left-hand edge of the high ground ahead of you, before swinging across the line of the ridge and then shadowing the slight bank of an old field boundary on your right downhill to another gate in a dip in the line of the ridge.

Through the gate, your path now passes just to the left of the small rocky knoll immediately ahead of you to pick up the fenceline on your right, which you now follow. Keep to this below the peaks of Bwlch-y-cefn bank, down the steep slopes of which you then drop to meet a track that passes along a cleft in the line of hills.

7 Turn right on the track, and immediately pass through a gateway. After a few hundred yards you pass through another gateway. As the track reaches the crest

of the rise, look for a small metal gate well over to your left, roughly in line with a block of conifer woodland beyond. Head for this gate across the intervening field and dug out streams. Once through the gate, keep following the line of the ridge through the gorse and tussocky grass (aiming for the left-hand edge of the conifer woodland) to another, wider metal gate. Go through this gate into a field, the path then heading between the fenceline on your left and the conifer plantation to another gate on the far side of the field. Through this it keeps to the left of another conifer plantation to cross the next field to another gate. Go through this, and the path heads towards the far left-hand corner of the next field to pass through a gate back onto the open hillside.

Your route back continues to another gate (or stile) ahead, but before crossing here, you may want to head up the hill to your right to see if you can fathom the remains of a hillfort.

LLANDEGLEY ROCKS HILLFORT
This Iron Age hillfort is comprised of two abutting enclosures measuring *circa* 200m long in total and 60m wide. Much of the site has been damaged by quarrying, so obscuring the original earthworks, but a possible hut platform some 6m in diameter lies near the junction of the two enclosures, and a possible robbed cairn *c.*4.5m in diameter has been identified near the centre of the site.

8 Once through the gate or over the stile, the now obvious track swings slightly left and slants downhill. When you meet a crossroads of tracks you turn right to follow the track to a house nestled in a group of trees. This is the house you almost reached when coming up the slope from the church, and once past it you take your original outwards route back to the church and where you parked.

9 If you want to visit the site of the spa and Trefonen mill, there is a slightly boggy path with one awkward stile you can take. Once back on the road on the far side of the church, turn right and walk down to the A44. Cross this and take the signposted footpath off to the left, which goes through a field gate set between the first small building reached on the left and a larger range of barns. The path follows the field boundaries on your

136

right, passing round some recent poultry sheds to reach an awkward stile crossing between two fields. (A gate has been placed across the stile, and the hedge is slightly overgrown.)

Once over the stile, aim for the corner of a number of posts that have been erected in the field (they may mark the course of a fence given time), and passing to the left of these posts, drop down to a footbridge across the Mithil brook. Join a track on the far side, and turn right to reach the old mill building.

Retrace your steps to return to the church and your car.

THE SPA

Beside the churchyard lies Burton House, a white-painted stone and timber building which possibly has 17th-century origins, though it became a 19th-century coaching inn at one time called the Burton Arms, and at another the Llandegley Inn. In 1854 this was rated as 'the only house [in] which a respectable visitor can find accommodation' in the village. In 1837, when Thomas Turner had stopped at the inn, he found it 'secluded and very comfortable … [and] chiefly occupied by a party of ladies, who were sojourning here for the benefit of the waters'. The inn had had a sunken bath installed in a downstairs room and adjoining rooms provided space for changing and for various treatments. A path led from the inn to Well House, constructed over the springs. This was just a few years after the waters were described as 'covered in a brown scum ….[having] an abominable stench …. but not an unpleasant taste'.

The sulphurous and chalybeate springs were in a field opposite the inn and about 100 yards on the other side of the turnpike road, now the A44. A building here accommodated a 'commodius bath'. In 1949 only a small derelict building in the middle of a field remained, and now there seems to be no sign of it.

This small spa was in vogue from the early years of the 1800s to the 1850s, visited for treatment of St Tecla's Disease (the falling sickness) amongst other ailments, when it was almost as famous as Llandrindod Wells, but then fell from favour.

Coal was once dug for locally, despite the comments of the geologist Sir Roderick Murchison, who predicted that no coal seams would exist.

Walk 19
Hundred House

7.75 miles on quiet roads, tracks and footpaths. The walk passes standing stones, the sites of a Roman camp and two Norman castles, and takes in the church at Llansantffraed-in-Elwel, in undulating countryside with no steep or long ascents. There is the occasional stile. The Hundred House Inn offers refreshment.

VILLAGE

After the demise of the two castles, the sites of which are seen on this walk, the settlement at Hundred House seems to have only just survived, in later years owing its existence to being on a drovers' route. Even then, in the mid 19th century, it consisted of no more than an inn, a chapel, a farm and another house around an area of common. Its name nevertheless shows it to have been the meeting place for the administration of justice in the hundred.

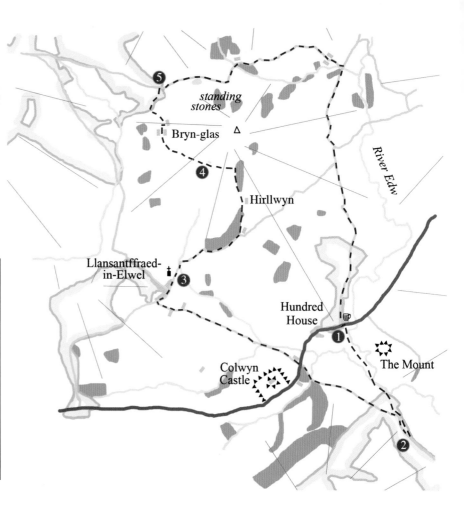

Park either at the Hundred House Inn if calling there before or after your walk, or at the small car park on the other side of the T-junction near the inn.

❶ Start by taking the footpath on the other side of the A road from the inn, going through a gate into a field between the upper reaches of the River Edw on the left and a house and barn on the right. Follow the field boundary on your left to a gate on the far side and then walk through the meadow beyond, shadowing the Edw on your left (and, as you start walking through the meadow, try to discern the tumulus on the rise in the field on your right).

TUMULI

Jonathan Williams in his history of Radnorshire written in the late 1700s and early 1800s recorded that within half a mile of Colwyn Castle were 'several tumuli or barrows, one on a small common near to the river Edw, in which were lately found two earthen jars, of known ware, curiously embossed, about 2ft high, closely covered with plain stones, and capable of carrying five gallons of liquid, and inclosing, originally, as it is supposed, human bones. These vases, on being exposed to the air, fell in pieces and the contents became dust and ashes, emitting an offensive smell, which continued for several days.' (For more on tumuli see pages 115 and 146.)

THE MOUNT MOTTE AND BAILEY

The castle that featured the large motte controlling the then crossing of the River Edw was probably begun around 1093 by Ralph Tosny of Clifford, taken by the Welsh under Madog ab Idnerth around 1135 and then rebuilt by Hugh Mortimer in 1144. Hugh probably lost the castle during the Anarchy and it was rebuilt by William de Braose in 1195. Either he or Hugh Mortimer appear to have built a shell keep in stone on the motte, but nevertheless the castle was taken and destroyed by Rhys ap Gruffudd in 1196. Colwyn Castle (see page 141) seems to have been built as its replacement.

The castle moat was fed by water from the Edw, then following a course closer to the castle site. The surrounding ground was so marshy that the castle bailey was formed by piling up gravel from the river bed.

Keep the Edw on your left, observing the motte of The Mount on its far side. You cross one ditch-cum-small stream about 50 yards up from its junction with the Edw and in due course reach the far end of the field at a junction of streams, where a bridge leads you over that which flows from the right. You now follow the smaller stream on your left (or possibly dry stream bed, depending upon the time of year), initially staying near the bottom of the bank on your right then rising up it a little, to leave the piece of woodland by a stile. After about 50 yards go through a field gate on your right, and then follow the old track slanting up the bank. You then follow this track (possibly best by walking along the top of the bank to its left) which roughly shadows the fenceline now below and to your left. As the track starts to once more near the fenceline it gains a more prominent and easier to walk along form and you follow it along the field boundary on your left to meet a road.

❷ Turn right on the road and follow it down to where it meets the A road. Cross over this and take the road on the other side, looking to the left to see the pink house on the site of Colwyn Castle (the Roman camp/castle site is more clearly seen from near where the road drops down to cross a stream a little further ahead). Follow the road up to a junction in Llansantffraed-in-Elwel, where you follow

COLWYN CASTLE

This site began its fortified life as a Roman marching camp delineated by a single bank and ditch and measuring some 180m square. The remains of this bank and ditch are most prominent on the south-western and south-eastern sides, for on the north-eastern side the motte of the Norman castle was built over it, whilst using the other banks to form the bailey. This castle seems to have superseded the one on the banks of the Edw and was probably begun *circa* 1200 by William de Braose when trying to wrest control of the area back from the Welsh as a new centre for the lordship of Elfael and centre of Colwyn Hundred.

It was probably taken from de Braose by King John in 1208, though it might have been taken by the Welsh in that year for it seems to have been in Welsh hands in 1215 and remained so during the rule of Llywelyn ab Iorwerth. On Llywelyn's death in 1240, the local Welsh leaders transferred their allegiance to Henry III and remained in possession. By the time of the rise of Llywelyn's grandson, Llywelyn ap Gruffudd, the castle was held by Sir Owain ap Maredudd from the Mortimers. When Llywelyn took the castle at Builth Wells, Sir Owain surrendered Colwyn Castle to him. He was nevertheless restored to English royal favour in 1276/7, only to, as misfortune would have it, rise with his sons in support of Llywelyn shortly before the latter's death in 1282. He therefore lost Colwyn Castle, which returned to the direct control of the Mortimers. The castle is mentioned in 1309 and 1337, but seems to have been abandoned by 1397. In 1563 a transfer of land simply refers to the 'site of Castle of Colwyne'. Some archaeological work was carried out in 1975 and 1982 which unearthed some Roman and medieval artefacts. The building that now occupies the site, Fforest Farm, was built in the 1620s and made use of some of the stone mouldings from the castle.

CHURCH OF ST BRIDGET, LLANSANTFFRAED-IN-ELWEL

The irregularly shaped churchyard may well enclose a smaller and earlier curvilinear church site. Whilst a Cistercian nunnery was founded at Llansantffraed before 1176 by an early abbot of Strata Marcella, near Welshpool, and possibly dissolved before 1186, its location has never been identified.

The church was described as being in a ruinous state before its restoration in 1895, and a picture in the church (reproduced here) shows what this building looked like; a dormer window over the porch might have been to provide light to a gallery. Elements of the walls were retained in the rebuild, but most of the structure dates from 1895. The late medieval font was retained.

Three embroidered panels by Jacqueline Jones depict St Bridget 'casting her light through the centuries'.

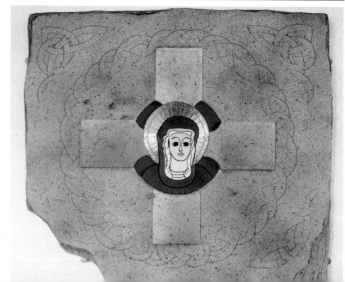

the road round to the right and then shortly afterwards keep straight ahead on a more minor road when the 'main' road bends left. After a couple of hundred yards you will come to the village church of St Bridget on the left, reached through a pair of impressive metal gates.

❸ The walk carries on along the road from the church till you reach a track off to the left just this side of a barn, leading to Hirllwyn farm. Take this track and keep to the left when it forks, and so pass to the right of a ruined barn and above Hirllwyn. Keep following the track and it will lead you uphill and alongside a small wood on your right. Near the crest of the hill, the track will curve away from the woodland and just after it starts to curl back on itself, you want to cross down to a field gate near a small pond on the opposite side of the ridge to that which you've climbed up.

❹ Once through the gate, follow the fence along on your right and cross another stile in this fence when you reach it (shortly before you would reach the corner of the field). Here the path diverges from the fenceline on your left. Initially aim for the right-hand end of a ridge on the horizon which has prominent scree slopes on its flank. As you cross over the rise in the field you will then see a gate near the far corner of the field for which you head.

Once through the gate, take the track which heads downhill through the next field and then to Bryn-glas farm. Keep on the track through the farmyard where you make a small dog-leg right and then left, to pass the farm bungalow on your right and thence over a cattle grid onto common land. Here you turn right to shadow the common boundary on your right and walk uphill to meet a small road.

5 Turn right on the road and keep an eye out for the standing stones on the hillside above a small lake that you soon pass. Keep on the road and follow it down and over a stream, and then on till you reach a T-junction. Here you turn right and follow the road to another T-junction, at which you again turn right. Then follow the road back to Hundred House, ignoring turnings to left or right.

Walk 20
Glascwm

7 miles largely on tracks with some quiet roads and footpaths, plus open hillside. This is a very hilly walk with one extremely steep ascent. There are also some stiles and one potentially awkward fence crossing. There are extensive views to be had and the possibility of finding (depending upon the state of the vegetation) an extremely small prehistoric stone circle.

Park near the T-junction in Glascwm.

1 Walk down the stem of the T-junction towards the stream, but carry on across the stream when the road bends left. You now follow a broad track up the hillside and above Cwm-Shenkin farm, the track subsequently dropping downhill to cross a stream. It then resumes an uphill course to reach the crest of the ridge, on which you will find the Giant's Grave.

Giant's Grave **2**

Cwm-Skenkin

Glascwm **1**

Penllanerch

3

Clas Brook

4

Rhos farm

River Edw

stone circle

tumulus **5**   **6**   *tumulus*

❷ Here you turn half left to walk up towards the crest of Little Hill. When the path soon divides, you can take either as they rejoin on the far side of the hill. After the paths have rejoined, the path descends more steeply downhill and swings to the right and heads towards a wind turbine. On the hillside below you are the a few house platforms, difficult to make out in the vegetation. As you near the wind turbine, the path swings left and drops down to a road.

❸ Turn right on the road, and when you reach the track that serves Penllanerch (the first track you come to off to the right), you want to go

GIANT'S GRAVE

When excavated, round barrows or tumuli such as the Giant's Grave are usually found to cover burials – either inhumations or cremations – placed within a pit or a stone-lined cist, the latter being more common in upland areas. Excavation can reveal that the barrows have been constructed on top of earlier structures, often represented by post holes, and sometimes they have a surrounding kerb of stones. Round barrows usually date to the Bronze Age (a barrow near Knighton excavated in 1935 yielded an urn dated *c.*1500BC), when the climate was such that the upland areas were more hospitable than they are now. The barrows are sometimes located on hilltops, but more often on the slope just below the hilltop, so that they appear to be on top of the hill when viewed from the valley below. On occasion, as with the Giant's Grave, they are constructed on a pass Barrows or tumuli have often accumulated folklore down the centuries, and the Giant's Grave is one such, for it is believed to be watched over by fairies.

through the gate opposite the track into the field on the left. A public path then follows the field boundary on your right down to the far right-hand corner of the field, where you go through a gate into the next field. The path now follows the field boundaries on your left, crosses a stile and so heads down to the road. Here you may have a fence to cross rather than a stile, but it should be free of barbed wire.

4 Turn left on the road and then right at the junction soon reached. Go through the gate on the left that you come to immediately before you would reach the buildings of the next farm (Rhos farm). The path crosses a small paddock to a gate into the field beyond. Here the path curves round the trees that stand above a small dingle and drops down to a footbridge across the Clas brook. Once over the bridge, head straight up the bank to a stile onto the open hillside. Turn right along the fence and where the path forks in a few yards, take the left-hand option and walk across and up the hillside, soon passing along a short section of fence to your right. When you reach the corner of the fence ahead, take a deep breath, for from you here you need to head up the hill. Zig-zag your way up the hillside, using sheep tracks, but returning to be close to the fenceline on your right as you head towards the crest of the ridge. Also keep an eye out for the small tumulus on a dimple of the ridge in the fields to your right. At the crest of the ridge you will find a wide grassy track.

5 Turn left onto the track, and presently it will level out for a while, before making another short rise, where there is a small amount of managed grassland on the upward slope off to the left. Keep an eye out here for a small pond on your left just a few yards from the track, which you should spot shortly before this short rise. To reach the stone circle you want to walk along the right-hand side of the pond (as looking at it from the path) and, keeping at an angle of 90 degrees to the path, head across the moorland for about a hundred yards. Depending upon the state of the vegetation you may be able to spot a small boulder. This is the most obvious remnant of a series of stones that circled a small bell barrow which will be to your left just before you reach the stone.

CEFN WYLFRE STONE CIRCLE
Only one stone is comparatively easily visible, but there are 12 small slabs and one larger boulder of volcanic origin. It is actually elliptical in shape rather than circular, measuring 23.8m by 22.5m.

6 Return to the track and continue along it. There are more tumuli off to the right as you pass the next height. Keep following the path into the saddle of the hill, and shortly after the track starts to rise again, take a path/track off to the left. This may be slightly obscure on the ground, but you are aiming for a path which skirts to the right of a cwm that drops away to your left. As you circle this cwm you will join a wider track on which you keep left. This will lead you in a gentle curve round and down the hill, leading you to the right of a small block of woodland out onto the road near Glascwm Church.

Turn right on the road to reach the church and then to return to where you parked.

GLASCWM AND THE CHURCH OF ST DAVID

It is thought that St David might have founded the monastery here which may have existed from the 6th century, though the church's dedication to St David can't be taken as proof of this. Nor can the belief that the 'Glas' in the name is derived from 'clas', the name given to early Celtic Christian settlements of monks, for others feel that 'Glas' is quite straightforwardly the Welsh for 'Green', with Glascwm simply meaning 'green valley'. Nevertheless, prior to the Norman incursions the church certainly seems to have been one of the most major in what became Radnorshire, and is still marked out as such by the size of its churchyard. In addition, in the mid 1200s the bishop of St David's made provision for building a house near the church 'in which he and his successors may be lodged'.

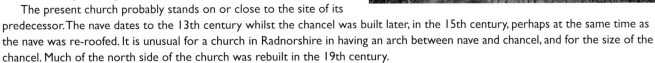

The present church probably stands on or close to the site of its predecessor. The nave dates to the 13th century whilst the chancel was built later, in the 15th century, perhaps at the same time as the nave was re-roofed. It is unusual for a church in Radnorshire in having an arch between nave and chancel, and for the size of the chancel. Much of the north side of the church was rebuilt in the 19th century.

In 1970 there was some ornamental panelling at the east end of the nave, marking the position where the rood loft had once stood but which was destroyed probably in the early 1800s.

There never seems to have been much of a nucleated settlement round the church, and in 1540 Leland mentions 'a chirche but few houses'. However there are extensive indications of house platforms or activity sites dating from the medieval period: earthworks in the field between the church and the village; a building platform and possible other features in the valley to the immediate north of the church and others on the north side of the stream; two or more platforms on the other side of the road to the south of the church and a third within the wood.

Wolves are reported to have lived in the area till the Tudor era.

In more recent times the village gained business from lying on a major drovers' route, and in the 1820s it had two inns: the Drovers Arms and the Radnorshire Arms. By the 1850s there were four inns, with the Carpenters Arms and Masons Arms also making an appearance. The drovers' route continued until the 1880s.

Walk 21
Rhulen

8 miles on a mixture of tracks, quiet roads and paths, with some stiles and a set of slightly awkward stepping stones, set in beautiful countryside alongside and above the River Edw. It includes meadows managed for their wild-flowers, two remote and particularly atmospheric churches, four bridges across the Edw and the mysterious Twm Tobacco's grave. There are a couple of stiff ascents.

Park near Rhulen Church.

❶ With your back to the gate into the churchyard, turn right and walk down the road, crossing the stream. Look out for the stile in the hedge on your left reached after about 200 yards beyond the stream and cross this into the field. The two meadows you are about to cross are managed as traditional wildflower meadows; mid June is the best time to see the majority of the flowers but the Common Spotted Orchid can be seen in April and May and early Purple Orchids near the old mill in the woods beyond.

Shadow the stream on your left to a stile in the field boundary on the far side. Cross this and then head towards the far left-hand corner of the field, but staying above the trees and the bank that drops down to the

CHURCH OF ST DAVID, RHULEN

Set in an originally sub-circular churchyard, this is one of the earliest church sites in Radnorshire. Old yews stand close by, suggestive of an early site, and it is said that in the 14th century another yew stood in the way of extending the chancel. Having said that, the existing building is difficult to date, but the original nave and chancel were probably built in the latter half of the 13th century. The east end was eventually extended, possibly in the 14th century but definitely before 1723, when it appears some restoration work was carried out. The west end was also extended, possibly not until the 18th century; the windows in this extension were subsequently blocked. It was re-roofed in 1961/2 and the west wall was rebuilt in 1985. The original entrance would have been through a doorway in the west wall, but this was replaced by the present south door probably in the 14th century, but possibly much later. The porch was reputedly added in the 17th century.

Inside, the east wall has an altar table cut into the thickness of the wall, above which is a moulded wooden beam with simple carved decoration that probably once supported a rood. The upper wall is also cut back to a similar width as the altar alcove creating a ledge on which, prior to the Reformation, visiting priests are said to have slept.

The ring on the church door to the left of the handle is an ancient sanctuary ring. From the Anglo-Saxon period onwards, those wanted for a crime or debt could claim sanctuary in a church for 40 days, so long as they could at least grab hold of the church's sanctuary ring before their pursuers could seize them. (This right was considerably reduced in the 16th century and abolished in the 17th.)

There has never been a nucleated settlement at Rhulen. In the mid 19th century just three houses stood close to the church, a pattern similar to that of today, with the parishioners scattered far and wide.

stream. Here you cross a stile into some woodland, and walk down to the stream where you will find the remains of a small mill. Immediately behind the near end of the mill you will find some not very obvious stepping stones across the stream (the OS map wrongly suggests a foot-bridge here). Use these to cross the stream, then turn right along the bank and after a few yards you will reach some steps that lead up the bank to a stile out into a field.

2 Once over the stile, turn right along the field boundary and this will lead to a grassy track that leads out of the field and between the woods that clad the slopes down to the stream on your right and a field on your left. Go through the gate at the end of the grassy track and join a stoned track on which you turn right. Just after the track has turned right to enter the farmyard of Cwmfillo, go through the double gates on the left just before a barn.

The path now follows the field boundary on your right, and you walk to the far end of the field, leaving it through gate into the next field; there may be some chickens in a small enclosure on your right near the gate. Cross this next small field, heading for a stile just to the left of a telegraph pole. Cross the stile and turn right on the road beyond.

3 Walk along the road, passing the entrance to Llanedw on your left and then carry on uphill for some 200 yards to where the road bends slightly right and a track heads off to the left. Go through the gate at the start of the track, and then take the second field gate on the left (reached after about 50 yards along the track). Initially the path stays on the high ground through the field, but it then drops downhill, crossing the field diagonally to the far right-hand corner. Here you cross a stile into the small paddock beyond, and turn immediately right to find a footbridge across the River Edw.

4 Cross the bridge and then turn left along the river and then right uphill, following the field boundaries. This will lead you to a gate into the next field, where the path turns slightly to the left and heads to the top left-hand corner of the field. Here you will find a gate out onto a road.

5 Turn left onto the road and follow it, ignoring a turning off to the right soon reached. Having passed Hergest farm it will lead you over a bridge across the River Edw. Turn right at the T-junction just across the bridge, and follow the road along and after about a mile over a bridge back across the Edw. Immediately over this bridge, go through the gate on the right and follow the river bank to another gate into the churchyard of Llanbadarn-y-Garreg.

6 Having visited the church, return to the road and turn right to continue along it and soon you will recross the Edw. Stay on the road as it slants uphill, and just after it bends slightly to the left, take the gravelled track

LLANBADARN-Y-GARREG AND ITS CHURCH

The simple single-celled church is first mentioned in 1291, and the structure has remained little changed since then. The building was restored in 1960 and the roof in 1992. The altar rails have been moved here from Aberedw Church and date from the 17th century, as does the pulpit. The rood beam survives and carries a faded painting of the royal coat of arms in place of the rood.

Earthworks in two fields between the river and the road through the village may represent medieval houses, whilst remains of buildings to the south-west of the church may have once been a drovers' inn, although the Edw valley has not been thought to have been a drovers' route. The ruins on the hillside above the church could be those of a chapel.

angled back on yourself for Pentwyn farm. Through the next gateway up the track, the footpath leaves the gravelled track and follows the hedge on the right up to the farm buildings, rejoining the track to pass through a gate into the farmyard.

7 Follow the track as it curves through the farmyard, passing one barn on your left and the farmhouse and other buildings on your right. Keep following the track and when it reaches a small piece of woodland, follow it round to the right and then left, so keeping the woodland to your left. At a gateway where the track ahead leads to a barn, turn right up a small track to another gate reached in about 100 yards. Go through this gate and follow the line of the track as it bends left and uphill. Thereafter keep straight ahead, ignoring one track off to the right. The track will eventually become more like a particularly well-defined sheep track, but keep on it. Near the summit you cross a track, but keep ahead and you will soon meet a more major track that runs approximately along the crest of the ridge. You should meet this track near a small dip in which lies Twm Tobacco's Grave.

TWM TOBACCO'S GRAVE

Kilvert tried unsuccessfully to find out who Twm Tobacco was, so the grave has existed since at least the 1860s. Several theories have been advanced: that he was a seller of contraband tobacco, killed for his wares; that he was connected with the Rebecca Riots against tollgates and shot by soldiers (but there would be no toll gates up on this stretch of hill); that he was a pipe-making shepherd who died in a fight with another shepherd; or someone who had built a ty un nos (a house built in a night which, if you had smoke rising from the hearth by dawn, would allow you squatter's rights) buried on his small patch of ground to save expense, but he would have been unlikely to choose a spot on the top of an exposed ridge for his house. Perhaps more likely is that he was a packhorse driver who was either killed for his wares and money, or simply died from exhaustion in bad weather.

8 Turn left on the track and follow it along. After about a third of a mile, another more major track joins it from the right and you keep along the combined track, soon dropping down into a major dip in the line of the ridge. Carry on up the far side and so to the next much slighter depression in the line of the ridge. Here you want to take the first track off to the left, to pass between a small pool and an outcrop of rock (see the photo on the right). Keep following the narrow track beyond the pool and this will lead you into a short narrow gully beyond which you meet another track.

Turn right on this track and at the junction of tracks soon reached, keep straight ahead, and straight ahead again at the next junction. Where the track splits further on, take the right-hand option and this will lead you down to a near-circle of stones which is a memorial to a Charles Letts. Apart from his name on one stone, the other stones are carved with the phrase: 'Your memory hallowed in that land you loved'.

Drop down to the gate below the memorial and so pass out onto a road. Turn left on this and head steeply downhill, turning right at the junction you reach to return to Rhulen Church.

Walk 22 Painscastle and Llanbedr

10.5 miles largely on tracks and quiet roads, with some footpaths. There is one stile. The walk takes in the strange feature called the Roundabout and two churches. Whilst many of the walks in this book have extensive views, this walk is hard to beat on this front. If timed right, the Roast Ox Inn can revive you at the end of a substantial walk.

Park near the Roast Ox Inn in Painscastle.

1 Walk down the road signposted to Clyro. As you descend the hill and walk towards the bridge across the river, keep looking out to your right for, in winter at least,

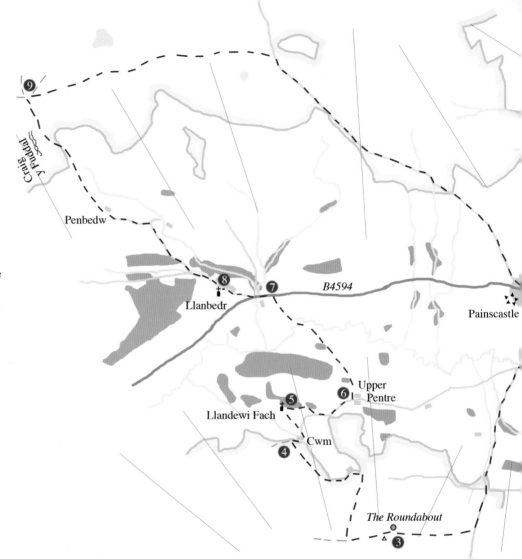

PAINSCASTLE

Named after its founder, Pain fitz John (a favourite of Henry I who became Sheriff of Hereford), it is therefore likely to date to 1120 at the earliest when it was built as the caput or military centre of the lordship of Elfael. Pain was killed in 1137 and the castle probably fell to Madog ab Idnerth (a descendant of Elystan Glodrydd, for whom see page 12) shortly afterwards. Ownership between Welsh and Norman may well have flip-flopped over the next few decades, but in 1195 Maud de Braose, of formidable renown, is credited with heavily defeating a Welsh force at Painscastle and the castle was subsequently rebuilt by her and her husband, William, the castle being known for a while as Castrum Matildis. Rhys of Deheubarth attempted to regain the castle the following year but without success. In 1198 Prince Gwenwynwyn of Powys led another assault on the castle but was repulsed with the help of a relieving force with heavy losses; some sources indicate 3,000 were killed but this is an improbably large number. Nevertheless, the story is included in Sir Walter Scott's novel *The Betrothed*, in which Painscastle is called 'la garde Douloureuse'.

The castle was taken from the de Braoses by King John in 1208, and probably held by a Welsh royal favourite until 1231 when Henry III decided to turn the castle into a major military base from which to harass the Welsh. Henry and his army stayed at the site for almost two months in the summer that year whilst the building work proceeded, a long time for the court to be static in one part of the kingdom and during which time, as one chronicler sarcastically noted, Llywelyn ap Gruffudd destroyed ten other castles. The court was kept busy however, for over 180 orders issued by the king during this period are still to be found in the records. Henry also seems to have established a town around the castle, as houses are mentioned in 1233, an annual fair and weekly market in 1264, and around 50 burgesses in 1309. In 1255 the castle was granted to Roger Tosny. In 1265, a year after Roger died, Llywelyn ap Gruffudd took the castle, but 12 years later it was rebuilt by Ralph Tosny. It was still defensible in 1401 when it was garrisoned against Owain Glyndwr, but by then the town was probably already in decay.

The 11m-high motte is still visible (notably in winter when the trees are bereft of leaves), and this probably supported a round tower. The entrance to the tower was via a barbican on the western side. The bailey to the north would have been surrounded by stone walls, which have now been grubbed up along with those of the tower and used in the surrounding buildings. The overall plan was that of a playing card, suggesting that it might have made use of the remains of an earlier Roman fort, an idea borne out by the reported finding of a Roman pavement on the site during the 1800s which was then reburied, its precise location not recorded. Upper House, in the group of houses just below the castle ramparts on the south-east, contains timbers probably dating from the mid 1400s (they were too charred from a fire to allow accurate tree-ring dating) of an aisled hall with cross wings that may have been the residence of the stewards of the Earls of Warwick, to whom the lands passed on the demise of the Tosnys. It was rebuilt in the 17th century.

you can gain a good profile of the earthwork remains of the castle.

② Once over the river, take the road off to the right, and then, almost immediately, bear left. Keep on the road uphill and it will lead you over a cattlegrid and out onto a common. Still keep to the road, passing a no through road off to the right, but before you reach the top of the ridge, take a grassy track off to the right that will lead you to the Roundabout, a stone wall encircling a copse at the summit of the ridge.

③ Having visited the Roundabout, carry on along the ridge, passing the trig point to your left. The track soon drops downhill slightly, heading towards a pond, but

---

THE ROUNDABOUT

The wall was originally constructed by the de Winton family of Maesllwch Castle (near Glasbury) to protect trees planted in 1887 to commemorate Queen Victoria's Diamond Jubilee. A combination of beetle attack, the Second World War's Home Guard or Royal Observer Corps using wood to keep themselves warm whilst spotting enemy aircraft, and a post-Second World War ice storm, led to a requirement for replanting. This took place in 1977, then in 1991 the common was given to the National Trust. The Roundabout was then restored to mark the new millennium, with two stiles provided to give access to the plantation and the new seat.

where it starts to flatten out, take the wide grassy 'track' (more like a wide gap in the bracken) off to the right. Pause a moment here and look roughly down the line of this 'track' for the roof of a small barn just beyond the far edge of bracken-clad common and this side of a tree: this is your target! As you descend the hillside it will disappear from sight for a while, and you will enter a maze of paths. So, target in mind, set off down the 'track' and keep roughly straight ahead as you enter the maze of paths, nevertheless probably needing to take one off to the left towards the edge of the common to find the barn. All being well, you should eventually find yourself walking along a major track, with the barn to your immediate right. Keep on this track and, once it has crossed a small stream, bear right when it forks. Follow this track and it will lead you downhill to meet a larger gravelled road.

4 Turn right on the road and go through the farmyard of the Cwm, from where the road gains a tarmacked surface. Just after you have passed alongside the end wall of the Cwm you come to a double gate ahead of you. Go through this and walk through the field aiming for the church ahead. You'll pass round the corner of a field that juts into the one you're in, but keep the line of telegraph poles to your left. Go through the gate into the churchyard to visit the church.

ST DAVID'S CHURCH, LLANDEWI FACH
The church was rebuilt in 1860 and nothing remains of the earlier structure. The building does have an unusual domestic fireplace in the nave, however. Ancient yews still stand in the churchyard, some looking as if they might once have formed part of a circle, and it is suggested that the site may have been chosen as a hermitage by one of the early Celtic saints. Some of the graves in the churchyard have taken up a variety of positions courtesy of badgers – the visitors' book in the church shows that spotting them has sometimes formed part of the joy of visiting the site. House platforms outside the churchyard indicate that the nearby settlement was once larger than the scattering of current farms suggests.

---

5 On leaving the church you can either return to the road by the same route, or, if feeling more adventurous (and able to cope with tall stinging nettles at the relevant time of year), leave the churchyard by the same gate, then turn left and take the small metal footpath gate to the right of a field gate into a field. Once in the field through stinging nettle alley, follow the boundary on your left to a gate into the next field. You cross this second field to a metal gate you can see on the far side to return to the road. Whichever route you've taken, turn left when you reach the road. Continue on the road up- and then downhill to reach Upper Pentre farm.

6 Here you turn left through a gate into the farmyard (opposite the farmhouse which is on the other side of the road), passing to the left of the barns, and then go through another gate and walk past the end of a small copse. In the field just past the copse, the path bends to

the left to head down to the far left corner, where a gate leads into the next field. Here you head for the right-hand end of another small copse near the foot of the downslope, where you will find a stile which you cross into the next field. Here you head to the far left-hand corner, just above the stream in the valley bottom. Take the right-hand of two gateways here and walk through the narrow piece of field just above the stream, to leave it by a bridge across the stream where you join a wide track. Follow this up to the B4594.

7 Turn left on the B road, and just over the bridge you soon reach, turn right onto another road. You'll soon reach Llanbedr Church on your left.

LLANBEDR

The earliest record of Llanbedr is in 1283, but the settlement only ever seems to have consisted of a church, the White House farm and a scattering of other farmsteads and cottages. The churchyard, however, being large and irregularly curvilinear with a low scarp bank to the south which has an ancient yew growing on it, suggests earlier Celtic Christian origins. The church has a 14th-century nave and a 15th-century chancel.

The vicar here between 1859 and the 1870s in Kilvert's time was Revd John Price, seen as something of an eccentric in Kilvert's writings. As there was no vicarage, Price initially lived in three bathing machines (as used in Victorian times to wheel women into the sea to maintain their privacy) until they burnt down, then a converted hen house. Known as the Solitary of Llanbedr, when Kilvert visited him in 1872 he found him living in a drystone walled hut, roofed in thin thatch. Kilvert wrote that 'the squalor, the dirt, the dust, the foulness and wretchedness of the place were indescribable, almost inconceivable'. (This 'house' lay in Cwm Ceilo, the cwm to the right of the one that this walk ascends to the ridge above Llanbedr, but nothing remains of it now.) At one point in his ministry, Price offered 5 shillings to each pair of vagrants living in sin who would come and be married. It was said that some, because Price's sight was so poor, took advantage of this offer several times.

8 From the church, continue on the road, soon reaching a no through road off to the right. Take this and follow it uphill, turning left when you reach a fork. This will soon bring into the farmyard of Penbedw farm. Keep ahead and you leave the far side by a gate that leads onto a track with field boundaries to each side. Follow this into the field ahead, where you keep following it, though now with just a fence on your right. At the far end of this field go through the right-hand of the two gates and shadow the field boundary on your left to the far end of the field, where this time you take the left-hand of two gates. This will lead you onto a grassy track which you follow uphill, past a quarry on your right and the crags of Craig y Fuddal on your left.

9 At the top of the rise you meet a track running along the ridge, and on this you turn right. Now you simply follow this along for a mile and a half, eventually meeting a road. You turn right on this and after a further couple of miles it will lead you back into Painscastle.

ROAST OX

Originally called the Maesllwch Arms, it was one of six inns in the Painscastle area that catered for drovers. It had its own smithy and provided accommodation for beasts at a halfpenny a head in a nearby field. It suffered a fire in the 1950s, when heavy snow prevented fire engines reaching the scene, and much of the top of the inn had to be rebuilt. In the 1980s it was renamed the Black Ox (to avoid confusion with a hotel of the same name in Glasbury), and in the early 1990s suffered from another fire which this time left just the porch and one wall standing. Rebuilt in the early 2000s, the name was changed to the Roast Ox in commemoration of the fire.

The triangular patch of grass fringed on all sides by roads to the south-west of the inn was the town's market place and probably lay at the heart of the medieval settlement. There is now a small public garden in the corner near the Clyro turn.

Walk 23
Aberedw

5.25 miles on tracks and paths with some quiet road. The walk includes the two castle sites at Aberedw together with the village's church, together with a circuit of the craggy hillside to the south. There is steady ascent to the top of the ridge, but no stiles. The Seven Stars can provide refreshment.

Park somewhere near the church and the pub, the Seven Stars, in Aberedw.

CHURCH OF ST CEWYDD, ABEREDW

The origins of the church may go back to the 6th century and to St Cewydd, the Welsh equivalent to St Swithin, with whom he shared the same Saint's Day, according to some sources, and on which day the weather can determine that for the next 40 days. The saint has only two other church dedications, at Disserth, also in Radnorshire and at Cusop, near Hay-on-Wye, in Herefordshire. A church is mentioned in documents for 1291. The nave was probably built in the 14th century, the porch (with its tiered benches used by mourners during wakes) in the 15th century, and the chancel in the 16th; the church may have had no chancel originally or a smaller one to that which is now present. A cage-like screen now separates off the chancel. It started life in the late 15th century as a standard rood screen with rood loft and tympanum above, but at some point in the 17th century these were taken down and replaced by the tiers of wavy balusters. In 1850s a school reportedly operated in the west end. Extensive restoration work was carried out in 1888, with further work in 1914.

❶ Enter the churchyard and take the path to the right of the church, leaving the churchyard by a stile in the corner. The path turns right along a fence, soon passing to the right of the motte of the first Aberedw Castle.

ABEREDW CASTLE I (right)

The motte perched above the Edw was probably begun in 1093 during the great Marcher advance into Wales, possibly by Ralph Tosny of Clifford or one of his Baskerville feudal tenants. Erosion of the mound has revealed a core of layered shale, suggesting that the tower on the motte might have been built of stone. There is no indication of any bailey, but one may have existed to the north. The castle had probably been destroyed by 1150, though it might have been rebuilt by a local Welsh princely family. If so, it was anyway ignored as the site for a castle in 1284 when Edmund Mortimer granted the land around to Walter Hackelutel, who built the other castle at Aberedw.

ABEREDW CASTLE II (above)

Walter Hackelutel received a licence to crenellate (essentially a licence to construct a castle) in November 1284, the grant suggesting that in fact Walter had already started its construction. Some of the money to pay for its building seems to have been arranged through loans from the then important Jewish community in Hereford. This new fortification was a square-style Edwardian castle, probably ditched all round, with round towers at each corner, that to the north-west seeming to be the largest. Its scale, though, resembled more a toy than a castle, a comparison supported by the thin layers of shale which seemed to have formed the walls. Walter retained what was perhaps more a fortified dwelling than a castle till his death in 1315, despite court proceedings by the Tosnys, who felt the lands were theirs by right, when it then passed together with the Tosny estates to the Beauchamp Earls of Warwick. They probably let the castle decay, for by the end of the 14th century it was declared to be worthless. The coming of the railway destroyed the western ditch and used much of the shale walling of the castle as ballast for the tracks.

The path then slopes downhill and towards the top of the steep-sided valley in which the Edw flows. It passes through two small gates, through the second of which it turns right through a field gate. The path then shadows the hedge on your right, passes through a gate to the left of some old sewage works and goes past some small barns to pass through another gateway to enter the crumbling stonework remains of the second Aberedw castle.

On the far side of the castle, don't follow the track down the slope but go through a gateway to the immediate right of the track and walk along a path that makes a dog-leg round a bungalow to bring you to a road. Turn right on this and walk back to the church.

2 Carry on past the church and in about a further quarter of a mile cross a bridge over the Edw. Take the road off to the right that you almost immediately reach, and follow this uphill. Where it loses its tarmac surface, keep to the right-hand track and follow it uphill. In due course it swings left and passes through a gate to emerge onto the open hillside, and almost immediately meets another track. Turn right on this track and follow it uphill, the track bending first right and then left before crossing another track. Keep on the track as it bends one way then another, but always heads uphill, crossing a sheep track and then emerging onto the crest of a broad ridge.

3 Almost immediately you meet a wide grassy track, on which you turn right and pass under overhead cables. Follow this track along and in due course it drops slightly downhill and leads you towards the bottom of a rocky escarpment where you will find a pool. From the pool, take the grassy track near the bottom of the escarpment,

and head downhill, keeping the escarpment to your immediate right. When you meet another track, turn right, and, after about 100 yards, right again when the track forks. (Near this fork, on the left-hand side of the track you don't follow, is a boundary stone on which is carved JRB 1882.) Keep following the track gently

downhill, keeping the crags to your right. Glimpses of the River Wye are to be seen in the valley ahead of you.

❹ In time the track will lead you into a cleft in the line of crags, whereafter it will take you along the edge of field boundaries on your left. You enter and leave one end of a craggy dell, still following the field boundaries on your left, and then drop downhill to meet a track near a derelict farmhouse. Turn right on the track and left when it meets another track after a few hundred yards. This soon meets a larger, gravelled, track, on which you turn

LLYWELYN'S CAVE

Some feel that the cave may have been used by druids before St Cewydd is said to have taken up residence for many years, but the cave is now associated with Llywelyn ap Gruffudd. Mystery surrounds Llywelyn's death and any part that the cave might have played in his life. Stories relate that during his campaigns against the Anglo-Normans in this part of Wales he sought sanctuary in the cave. More likely it could have been the rendez-vous point in December 1282 when, according to some suggestions, the Mortimers, who were related to Llywelyn, lured him away from his army, which had been brought south for an assault on Builth Castle, with promises of assistance, only to have him killed. Other accounts of the events of 11 December 1282 talk of a battle near a river crossing where Llywelyn's forces were routed, the prince and a small group of men being pursued and killed as they tried to escape; only afterwards was Llywelyn's body recognized. Whatever the chain of events, his head was sent first to Builth, then to Edward I who was then at Rhuddlan, whilst his body was buried at Cilmeri, where a stone commemorates the spot, before being reinterred at Abbeycwmhir.

left and this will lead you to a second derelict farmhouse. Go through the gate by the side of this farmhouse and follow the track all the way downhill. Llywelyn's cave lies in a small rocky escarpment off to the left which you soon pass round the end of, but is not reached by a public footpath.

5 A little later the track makes a sharp right-hand turn and drops down to meet the road on which you began the ascent of the hill. Turn left, and left again at the junction soon reached to return to Aberedw.

Walk 24
Erwood

4 miles on a mixture of tracks, paths and quiet roads, but with one steep descent that can rely on finding sheep tracks, particularly awkward in the seasons of flourishing bracken. There is also a fairly steep ascent at the start of the walk. There are no stiles. The walk includes the church at Llandeilo Graban and the various earthworks and tumuli at the top of Twyn y Garth, where there is also a German field gun. Tea and recovery time can be had at the Erwood Station Gallery if you time it right.

Park at the car park next to Erwood Station Gallery (and tea room).

1 Turn right out of the car park entrance along the road, almost immediately turning left up a tarmacked lane, and then after about 100 yards left again, onto a path-cum-track which leads up and across the hillside. It soon appears to be heading towards a rock outcrop, but actually bears to its right. Immediately over the crest fork right to reach a gate which leads out onto a road. Turn right on this and follow it along to the entrance to the churchyard at Llandeilo Graban.

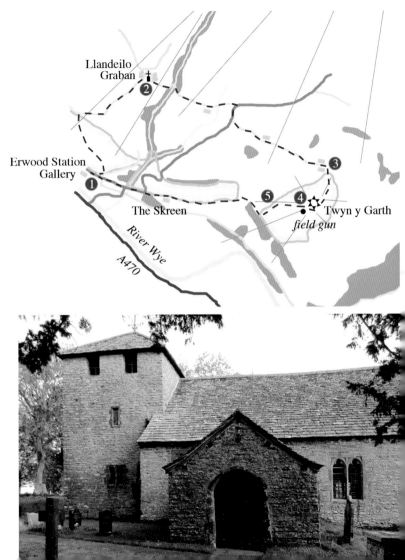

CHURCH OF ST TEILO, LLANDEILO GRABAN

To the north-east of the church the names of some buildings and pools incorporate the word 'henllan', meaning old church, suggesting that the original church stood somewhere in that direction. The current church is known to have existed in 1291, but the nave dates from the 14th or 15th century, the chancel and porch probably from the latter century. In 1818 the chancel was separated from the chancel by a timber screen which was removed in the Victorian era. Some restoration was carried out in 1897.

To the west and south-west of the church lies a network of fields running west-north-west to east-south-east and showing aratral curves in their alignment. (These curves are difficult to see from any vantage point on the walk, but they can be seen on the OS Explorer map – if you have that with you.) Such 'reversed-s' curves were formed due to the medieval ploughman beginning to turn his team of cumbrous oxen before he reached the headland at each end of the field. Such fields suggest a scale of agriculture which would have required a greater workforce than is represented by the surviving dwellings.

In the early 1900s, the Revd D.E. Owen recorded a story he had heard about the last dragon in Radnorshire:

'Ages ago, one of these vicious and powerful brutes slept every night on the tower of Llandeilo Graban Church, after making dreadful devastation during the day. Many brave men tried to destroy the monster but their attempts were always futile, and sometimes even fatal to themselves. At last, the parishioners offered a rich reward to anyone who would capture and slay this destructive brute, which measured three yards and one inch long. After many vain attempts on its life it became 'curster' than ever. An ingenious plough boy, attracted by the handsome reward, devised a plan that proved successful. He made a dummy man out of a large log of oak, and, aided by the local blacksmith, armed it with numerous iron hooks, powerful, keen and barbed. Then he dressed the dummy in red and fixed it firmly on top of the tower. At dawn the following day the dragon first saw his daring bedfellow and dealt him a violent blow with his tail, which was badly torn by the hooks. Infuriated by the pain he attacked the dummy with tooth, claw, wings and tail, and finally wound himself round his wooden foe and bled to death.'

❷ Your route continues through the churchyard and out of its other entrance on the far side from where you entered, through a small car park and back to a road, on which you turn right. Follow this along, and in about half a mile you reach a T-junction. Turn right and then take the no through lane off to the left reached in a couple of hundred yards and signposted to Garth. Follow this along and in another half mile or so you'll come to a group of houses.

TWYN Y GARTH

The origins of a castle are obscure, and it might have only been occupied for a few years. Possibly built by Marcher lords c.1208/10, it was probably abandoned by 1215. Alternatively, it might have been a Welsh castle, built either by Einion Clud (k.1177) or Cadwallon ap Madog (k.1179).

The main remnant of the castle is a ringwork near the summit of the hill. The ringwork is *circa* 112 feet in diameter, with an entrance on the east. To the south of the ringwork, the possible bailey rampart with slight outer ditch is roughly rectangular in shape and slopes downhill. It is possible that this just represents the marking out of a bailey, such as would have occurred at other castle sites, but that it was never actually built. Further to the south is a stretch of bank and ditch 108 feet in length. Two small mounds some 600 feet away to the north-east of the ringwork are probably tumuli. Other depressions and hollows could relate to the castle, or be the works of the Home Guard or the Americans during the Second World War. Between the ringwork and the First World War gun are the foundations of what could have been a small rectangular building. At certain times of the year bracken might obscure your ability to see some of these features.

The gun itself is a German light field howitzer. Advertised for sale by the War Office after the end of the First World War, it was bought by Nessa Williams Vaughan (later Mrs Lionel Trafford) of Llandeilo Graban in memory of her brother, killed during the Battle of the Somme, and of other local men killed in the war. It arrived at Erwood Station in 1920 and was dragged up the hill and concreted in place – and then suffered from corrosion for the next 80 years to become the focus of a millennium restoration project.

3 Just past the first house on the right, look for the sign to 'Garth Common' and to 'the gun'. Take the track indicated, keeping two houses to your right, and enter the 'yard' of the second house. Cross this and take the grassy track up to a gate onto the common. Take the track ahead, which slants up the hillside, and this will lead you in a gentle 'S' to a German field gun, itself near the earthworks which circle part of the summit – or, when bracken cover allows, cut across and up the hillside direct to the remains of the earthworks. The earthworks are the remains of Twyn y Garth castle and a couple of tumuli. Even if the hillside is well covered in bracken, the crest of the ramparts are fairly free of the plant, allowing you to walk around the feature. The tumuli can be seen from the ramparts in profile against the hills behind.

4 The next bit of the walk can be difficult, especially when the hillside is covered in bracken, for you need to descend the hillside to

pick up a track that runs at the foot of the common; this is obviously easier the less there is of a bracken entanglement. The 'best' route is to take a bearing off the field gun: looking along the muzzle, you want to pick a route down the hillside to its right (there may be one just to the right of the line of the muzzle, and another further to the right). Take what paths and sheep tracks you fancy and head down to the bottom of the common, where you will find a track running along its north-western boundary.

5 Turn left on this and follow it along till you come to a gate on your right, with an area of recently felled woodland ahead of you. Go through this gate and follow the track to join, in a bit over half a mile, the drive to a house called The Skreen. Keep right on this and follow it to its junction with the B4594, on which you turn left. When you meet the B4567 to Aberedw, turn right to return to the gallery.

Walk 25
Llanstephan

3.25 miles on a mixture of tracks, footpaths and quiet roads. There is a stiffish short ascent to Ciliau, and another gentle ascent, but this is a fairly short

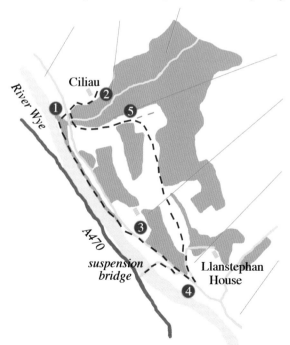

and relatively flat walk compared to many in this book. It includes a good length of track close to the banks of the Wye. The only stile you have to cross is that by the layby where you park.

On the road between Boughrood and Aberedw you cross a bridge with metal railings on what was the railway line and marked 'Weak bridge 7.5 tons'. Park in the layby just to the north (the Aberedw side) of this bridge.

❶ At the bridge end of this layby you'll see a stile in the fence, which you cross and head down some steps to join a track. Turn right on this and then almost immediately left onto another track, and follow this up alongside the fence bordering some woodland on your right. This will lead you into the farmyard of Ciliau.

CILIAU

The house dates from the first half of the 16th century, though that structure may itself be the reconstruction of an earlier cruck-trussed hall house. It was probably built by Robert ap Gwilym, chief constable of Painscastle Hundred in 1552-53, who claimed descent from Prince Rhys ap Tewdur of Deheubarth (south-west Wales). The main entrance leads into the central hall, a large fireplace to the right of the door being built at the same time, for there is no evidence of any smoke blackening on the roof timbers, which would have been the case if, initially, there had been an open hearth in the middle of the hall. To the right of the fireplace (as you look at the building across the yard from the path) was a passage, floored over to provide a semi-gallery overlooking the hall. Beyond the passage was the kitchen. On the left of the building as you look at it would have been a parlour. The upper storeys are timber-framed and with the roof alignment give the appearance of an H-plan house, when in fact it is rectangular.

2 Having enjoyed looking at the fine building from the track, return down it, pass under the old railway bridge and cross the footbridge over the stream. Go through the gate ahead and then keep left, to follow the path that stays close to the banks of the Wye on your right. This will eventually lead you out onto the Boughrood to Aberedw road.

184

SUSPENSION BRIDGE
This was built in 1922 by David Rowell and Co, a company formed in London in 1855. The company initially traded as a fencing business but diversified into structural steel frame buildings and bridges, erecting a number of small suspension bridges. The company went into liquidation in 1970.

❸ Turn right on the road, and when you reach a turning off to the right, take this road and follow it down to see the narrow suspension bridge across the Wye and stretches of the river, then return back up to the Boughrood and Aberedw road and turn right.

❹ Very shortly you'll come to the curving stone wall and white gate marking the entrance drive to Llanstephan House. Go through the gate and walk up the tarmacked

drive. After about 200 yards go through a small metal gate on the left into some recently cleared woodland. Through the gate, immediately turn right and shadow the drive to another small gate which leads into a field.

There are two paths here; the one you want is the right-hand one, which shadows the field boundary to the right, several yards into the field and passing just to the left of a lone tree. The path curves gently to the left and rises uphill, following the field boundary on your right. Near the crest of the hill you pick up a fence on your left, which you follow to a gate into the next field. Once in this field, follow the edge of woodland on your right round to the next field gate. Once through this gate the path gently diverges from the woodland boundary on your right to head to a gate at its far end, just above the woodland that is on your left; the gate is invisible in a dip in the ground until you are very close to it. Through this gate, the path curves gently to the left, heading towards a gate to the right of some conifer woodland.

5 Here you will join a track on which you turn left to go through the gate. Once through, however, you want to bear slightly right off the track to follow a faint grassy path heading downhill that diverges slightly from the course of the track, passing just to the left of a lone Scots Pine and then to the right of a wooded bank. Beyond the bank, the path initially keeps to the left of the trees on your right, then passes to the right of four large oaks to reach a metal gate and stile in a fence. Once over the stile or through the gate, follow the obvious path down to another gate and go through this. Follow the stream on your right and then cross the footbridge to return to your vehicle.

Walk 26
Maesyronnen and Llowes

5.25 miles largely on footpaths with some quiet roads and tracks. The walk is set in undulating countryside with no great hills to climb, but there are several stiles. The walk includes the unusual Maesyronnen Chapel and Llowes Church with its Celtic cross.

Park at Maesyronnen Chapel. This you can visit at the end of your walk, having collected the key in Ffynnon Gynydd (if doing your walk in 'normal working hours' as the key is collected from a metal fabricator's).

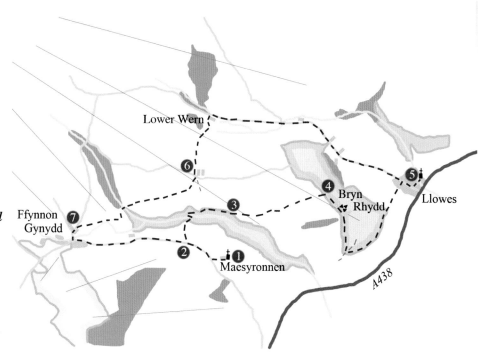

❶ With your back to the chapel, turn right and head for the left of the two field gates at the other side of the parking area. Through the gate, follow the hedge on your right, and cross the stile at the end of the field, emerging onto a lane. Turn right along the lane.

❷ Past a bend in the lane, cross a stile by the side of a gate on the right. Walk alongside the fence on your

right to the far side of the field. Here you will find a stile which you cross to enter a wood. The path curves round the valley side and takes you down to a bridge across a stream, and then up the other side of the valley. Near the far side of the wood your path will cross another, and here you turn right. In a couple of hundred yards you cross a stile into a small clearing with the remnants of a small farm. Pass between the buildings and cross another stile

back into the woodland. Carry on along the path which follows the edge of the wood, and eventually leads you out over a stile into a field.

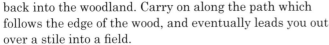

3 Turn right and walk above the lower corners of the field to a stile in the fence at the end of the field, then walk across the next field, bearing slightly left, to another stile. Over this stile, turn left along the hedgerow and go through the first gate you reach. Head across this field aiming for the fir tree to the left of the house on the ridge. Cross a stile and head to another stile on the far side;

cross this into a small 'paddock' and then cross another stile out onto a track and so out through a gate onto a minor road on Bryn yr Hydd Common.

4 Turn right on the road. Where it bends to the left, take the path indicated to the right and downhill, but first notice (if you can amongst the bracken) the ditch and banks on your left at this corner indicating the site of the Bryn Rhydd enclosure.

BRYN RHYDD ENCLOSURE

An area of roughly 140m by 95m has been partially enclosed by a bank that now stands up to half a metre above the interior and 1.5m above the base of an outer ditch. Of probable Iron Age date, it might represent the boundaries of the buildings comprising a farmstead, subsequently partly obscured by later field systems.

Keep following the path till it meets a bridleway near the bottom of the common on which you turn right and then almost immediately (i.e. after about 5 yards) left onto the Wye Valley Walk. This path will lead you through the woodland at the foot of the common, and out into a field by a small gate. The path crosses this field, aiming for a corner in the fence straight ahead, to then pass alongside a strip of fence on your left and through a series of gates out onto a road. Turn right and take the second no through road to the left to reach the church of St Meilig (see overleaf).

❺ After visiting the church, retrace your steps along the no through road and thence to the 'main' road and turn right, soon passing the path you recently walked along. Continue along the road; at the edge of the village there's

CHURCH OF ST MEILIG, LLOWES

St Meilig was reputedly the son of Caw, prince of the British kingdom of Strathclyde, and brother of the historian monk, Gildas, who moved south after being driven off his lands by the Picts and the Scots c.650 AD. Initially a warrior, Meilig then sought a religious life, and after studying (either with St Cybi on the Arran Islands, or with St Cadwg in Glamorgan) founded a monastic community near Llowes. Here he might have joined a St Llywes or Lyuhes who was to give his name to the subsequent settlement, though, alternatively, this may be derived from the old Welsh *lloches/llochwes*, meaning a refuge. In the 12th century there is a reference to an anchorite by the name of Wechelin having a hermitage here.

The lower part of the church tower is perhaps medieval, but the rest of the church, with the exception of parts of the walling, dates to a rebuild in 1853-5 under the architect W.J. Worthington. The font was retained, but the joy of the church is the monolithic stone with carvings of two crosses that stands at slightly under 7 feet tall, though its full length is some 12 feet, its base tapering to a chisel-like point. Below what is now visible, the stone has been described as having a band of relief on the two main faces that provided a shelf on which smaller crosses or offerings may have been put. The carved stone was only moved into the church in 1956, having first stood at Croesfeilig at the junction of the parishes of Llowes, Clyro and Llanddewi Fach, then being moved into the churchyard during the 12th century. The stone is sometimes referred to as the Moll Walbee stone, named after Maud de Braose. She had a fearful reputation in real life, leading an army against the Welsh, and in later years was credited with several supernatural doings. These often assumed she was of the build of a giant and so was able to carry stones in her apron from which to build Hay Castle in a single night. One of these stones supposedly fell into her shoe; she picked it out and in anger threw it across the Wye, where it landed in Llowes churchyard.

On what is now the eastern face is a wheel-cross of Latin type but carved in a Celtic pattern in, it is thought, the 11th century; on its western face is a more stolid cross with no decoration, believed by some to have been carved in the 6th or 7th century and by others at the same date as the Celtic-patterned cross. On the north side is a shield-shaped panel.

The settlement always appears to have been small. In 1816 Llowes consisted of the church, the Radnor Arms inn (on the other side of the main road and only recently closed), a mill and nine houses. The Old Vicarage incorporates a cruck-framed hall of late 16th-century date or earlier, while the previous inn contains a main range said to date variously to somewhere between the 15th and 17th centuries. Possible house platforms nearby indicate that the settlement may have been a little larger at some point in the past.

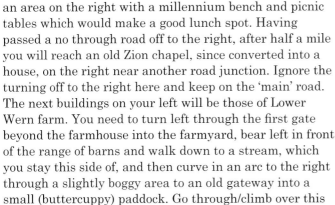

an area on the right with a millennium bench and picnic tables which would make a good lunch spot. Having passed a no through road off to the right, after half a mile you will reach an old Zion chapel, since converted into a house, on the right near another road junction. Ignore the turning off to the right here and keep on the 'main' road. The next buildings on your left will be those of Lower Wern farm. You need to turn left through the first gate beyond the farmhouse into the farmyard, bear left in front of the range of barns and walk down to a stream, which you stay this side of, and then curve in an arc to the right through a slightly boggy area to an old gateway into a small (buttercuppy) paddock. Go through/climb over this

gate and cross the paddock to a gateway on the far side. Go through this (and over the small stream) to find yourself in a much larger field. Cross this diagonally to the far top corner where you'll find a gate that leads onto a track. Go through the gate and down the track, through another gate and on down the track to meet a road.

6 Turn left on the road and fairly immediately you will come to a gate/stile on the right which you want to go through/cross. Once in the field, head for a point straight ahead, about 50 yards to the left of the far right-hand corner, where a stile will lead you into the next field. Once over the stile, turn right and follow the field boundary

FfynnonCynidr

Erected
in loving memory of
Walter Fenwick
de Winton
Aged 27
Who died in Central Africa
March 28. 1892
serving God his Country
and his fellow men

Draw water out of the
wells of salvation

along, crossing another stile in the corner of this field. Again follow the field boundary along on your right till you reach a gate on the right about 100 yards from the end of the field. At this point you want to bear left and head across the field to find a track that takes you down to a bridge which you take across a stream. Head up the bank on the other side. At the top you want to cross the field ahead of you, aiming initially to pass just to the left of a couple of old willows that stand in the field, beyond which you should see a stile at the junction of a length of hedge to its left and fence to its right. Cross this stile and head across the next field aiming for a gateway to the right of a red brick bungalow behind a stone wall on the far side.

7 Through the gate turn left on the road, then left again at the junction ahead. You'll soon reach Ffynon Cynidr on the right, under a rustic looking shelter.

> ### FFYNNON CYNIDR OR ST CYNIDR'S WELL
> Known as a wishing well, sometime between 1900 and 1910 the well-house was built and the earlier well-chamber partially covered. There is a memorial plaque to Walter Fenwick de Winton, of the de Winton family of nearby Maesllwch Castle, who in 1892 died of fever in what is now Uganda and is buried in the grounds of Kampala's Anglican cathedral.

You now need to decide whether you wish to collect the key for Maesyronnen Chapel. If you do, turn right at the junction ahead and ask for it at the new barn which houses a forge; remember you'll have to drive back at the end of the walk to return it. (It is possible to gain an impression of the chapel by looking through its windows, but it does repay an actual visit.) Having collected the key, about face and walk down the lane, passing the junction from which you recently emerged.

If you don't collect the key, instead turn left.

In either case, after about half a mile, during which you'll pass the footpath to the left which you took at the start of the walk, the road bends to the right. Keep an eye out for a stile on the left which is well hidden in the hedge. Cross this stile (which you also used in your outward journey) and follow the field boundary on your left to return to the chapel.

MAESYRONNEN CHAPEL

An Independent religious community formed locally in the 1640s as an offshoot of the Baptists of Llanigon and Hay. They probably soon began to use the barn that became Maesyronnen Chapel as their place of worship. With the Restoration of the monarchy in 1660, worship outside the Church of England had to be practised with a degree of secrecy until the Act of Toleration of 1689 allowed the community to practise their faith openly. Maesyronnen Congregational Chapel, as the worshippers called themselves, was formed in 1692 and the barn was converted to a chapel five years later. It is the oldest surviving nonconformist chapel in Wales by some 80 years. The chapel was refurbished around 1985 and again in 2007/8. The internal furnishings retain many of their 18th- and 19th-century features, including box pews, a pulpit and memorials, together with a large oak table still used for communion services. On the wall near the pulpit is a certificate in recognition of funds raised by the congregation for a missionary schooner in 1930.

The adjoining cottage was built in the early 1700s. The last tenant left in 1979 and it is now in the care of the Landmark Trust and can be rented as holiday accommodation.

Both R.S. Thomas and Roland Matthias were moved by their visits to the chapel to write poems, each entitled 'Maesyronnen', expressing the feelings their visits engendered.

Index (**bold** page numbers denote the subject of boxed information)

Abbeycwmhir 19-24, 176
  Abbey 19, **20-21**, 131
  Church of St Mary **19**
  Dyfaenor **23**
  Hall **22**
  Happy Union inn **24**
Aberedw 169-176
  Castle I **170**
  Castle II **172**
  Church of St Cewydd 153, **170**
Ailesbury, Earl of 92
Alcock, Leslie 7
America 123
archaeology 7-8, 10, 109, 139, 141
Arthurian legend 51
Athelstan, King 12

Bachefeld, William and Flory 111
Badlesmere, Elizabeth de 73
Bailey Einon Nature Reserve **15**
Baldwin, Archbishop 103

Bank of the Black Ox 45
barrows, see tumuli
Bedd Garmon 32
Beilibedw Mawn Pool 115
Bellamy, David 6
Black Death 60, 98, 103
Black Yatt 116, 117
Bleddfa 64-67
  Castle **67**
  Church of St Mary Magdalene **65**
  Hundred House Inn **67**
  Trust 65
Bohun, Humphrey de 12
Bradshaw family 86
  John 99
Brampton, Brian de 58
Braose, de, family 57, 58, 109, 119
  Philip de 109
  Matilda de 39
  Maud de 159
  William de 101, 109, 120, 140, 141

Bridget, Saint 142
Bronze Age 146
Brownlow, Kevin 116
Bryn Rhydd enclosure **189**
Bryn y Castell 58
Bryn y Maen 114, **115**
Burlinson, James 89

Cadwallon ap Madog 20
Cam Nant Roman Camp **33**
Carausius 8
Cascob 74-79
  Church of St Michael and All Angels **77-78**
  Dyffryn 74
Castell Foel-Allt 72, **73**
Castell Tinboeth 38, **39**
Castell y Blaidd **47**
Celts 32, 131, 149, 162, 163, 190
Cefn y Crug Cross Dyke **128**
Cefn Wylfre Stone Circle **147**

Cefnllys 11-18
  Alpine Bridge 18
  Bailey Einon Nature Reserve **15**
  Castle **12-13**
  Church of St Michael **14**
  Old Castle **18**
  Pentre mound 16
Cewydd, Saint 170
Chandos family 57
  Roger 57
Charlemagne 85
churchyard, circular 14, 32, 151
Civil War 21, 30, 109
Clud, Einion 120
Constantius Chorus 8
Crusade, First 103
Cynllo, Saint 25

Davies, Andrew 55
dissolution 21
Ditch Bank 128
Domesday Book 69, 80, 101
dragons
  Dragon's Tooth 51
  Fabulous Water Beast 1

  last dragon in Radnorshire **180**
drovers
  inns 24, 153, 168
  roads **44-5**, 138, 149

Ednol
  Church **76**
Edward I, King 71, 176
Edward II, King 39
Edward IV, King 87
Elan Valley Trail 29, 30
Elfael 120
Elye, William fitz 105
Erdington, Thomas 57, 58
Erwood 177-182
  Station Gallery 177
Esgairperfedd 33
Evans, Edward Middleton 5

Felindre 43-48
Fenton, Richard 7
Fforest Inn 114, **121**
Ffynnon Cynidr **192**
First World War 36, 181
Fletcher, H.L.V. 121
folklore 32, 51, 55, 78, 104, 146, 180, 190

Four Stones, the **104**, 105
Fowler family 21
  Richard 19, 23
Fraxino, de, family 101

Geneville, Joan de 73
Gerald of Wales 27, 32
Giant's Grave **146**
Gibbs, John 103
Gilfach Nature Reserve **34**
Glascwm 145-149
  Church of St David **149**
  Giant's Grave **146**
Glastonbury Thorn 89
Glodrydd, Elystan 12, 111, 120, 159
Glyndwr's Way 22, **43**, 62
Gogyrfan, giant 51
Green
  Margaret 58
Green Price, Sir Richard 58, 60, **83**, 87
Grey of Ruthin, Lord 71
Greyndour, Sir John 109

Grinshill stone 21
Griwallt ap Llechitwyt 6
Grosvenor, Mr 5
Gruffudd ap Llywelyn 98
Guinevere 51
Gwenwynwyn of Powys 159

Hackelutel, Walter 172
Hardinge, George 92
Harley family 101
Hatton, Sir Charles 99
Hay Castle 190
Helen, mother of Constantine 25
Henry I, King 159
Henry II, King 57, 120
Henry III, King 13, 20, 101, 105, 141
Henry IV, King 71, 109
Hoare, Sir Richard Colt 7
Hook, Rolf 51
Horne, William 87
house platforms 13, 47, 76, 105, 110, 117, 135, 146, 149, 162, 190
Howse, W.H. 119

Hugh the Donkey 57, 80
Humperstons, the 22
Hundred House 138-144
  Colwyn Castle 140, **141**
  history **138**
  Mount Motte and Bailey **140**

Iron Age 189
Isolda 105
It Happened Here (film) 116

Jellicoe, John 36
Jewish community, Hereford 172
John, King 20, 57, 101, 109, 141, 159
Jones, Jacqueline 142
Julius Frontinus 8

Kempson, F.R. 30
Kerry Ridgeway 44
Kilvert, Francis 32, 155, 163
Kinnerton **105**
  Castle 105
  Court 105
  St Mary's Church 105

Knighton 56-63, 83
  Almshouses **58**
  Castles **57-58**, 61, 63
  Chandos House 60
  Church of St Edward **59**
  clock tower 60
  history **60**
  Horse and Jockey 60
  Norton Arms Hotel 60
  Offa's Dyke Centre 56, 63
  trade 60
  Wylcwm Street 58
Knights Hospitaller 119
Knucklas 49-55
  Castle 49, **51**
  Community Land Project **50**
  Old Red Lion **54**
  Viaduct **49**, 50

l'Asne, Hugh, see Hugh the Donkey
Leland, John 13, 80, 109
Letts, Charles 157
Lewis family 111

Lewis, Sir George Cornewall 83, 103
Lewys Glyn Cothi 13, 25
Llananno
  Church of St Anno **41**, 42
Llanbadarn y Garreg Church **153**
Llanbedr
  church **163**
  history **163**
Llanbister 25
Llandegley 130-137
  Burton House 137
  Church of St Tecla **131**
  Rocks Hillfort **135**
  Spa **137**
  Trefonen mill 136, 137
Llandeilo Graban
  Church of St Teilo **179**
Llandewi Fach
  St David's Church **162**
Llandrindod Wells 1-10, 98
  Bach y Craig farm 5
  Baptists' oak 3
  Capel Maelog **10**

Castel Collen 3, **7-8**, 10

chalybeate spring 7

Church of the Holy Trinity **2**

County Hall 5

dragon fountain 1

Eye Well 7

history **5**

Llandoddies 6

Llandrindod Hall 5

Lovers' Leap 3

Pump House 5, 9

railway 9

rector of 14

Rock Park 3, 5

Spa **5**, 83

wells 6, 7

Llanfair Waterdine 54

Church **55**

Davies tombs **55**

Llanidloes Church 21

Llansantffraed Cwmdeuddwr 26, 27

Church of St Bride **30**

Llansantffraed-in-Elwel 141-142

Church of St Bridget **142**

Llanstephan 183-186

Ciliau 183, **184**

suspension bridge **185**

Llanvihangel 112-121

Church of St Michael **119**

Great House 119

Red Lion **119**

Llowes 189-191

Church of St Meilig **190**

lluests **116**

Llynheilyn (lake) 112, **114**, 121

Llywelyn ab Iorwerth 20, 21, 27, 58, 109, 120, 141

Llywelyn ap Gruffudd 12, 21, 39, 51, 58, 60, 80, 101, 109, 159

Llywelyn's Cave **176**

Mabli, Abbot 19

Madog ab Idnerth 140, 159

Maelienydd 12, 20, 27, 73, 120

Maesllwych Castle 92, 160

Maesyronnen 192-194

Chapel **193**

Margeria 105

Martin, Richard 98

Mathias, Roland 193

Meurig ab Ade 120

Meurig Barach 120

Millbank, Powlett 87

mining 123, 137

Moelfre City **40**

Mollo, Andrew 116

Montfort, Simon de 109

Montgomery, Treaty of 12, 13

Morgan, Mary **92**

Mortimer family 12, 20, 27, 39, 47, 51, 57, 58, 73, 87, 101

Edmund 71, 73

Hugh 140

Maud de 111

Ralph 18, 58

Roger (I) 18

Roger (II) 12, 13

Roger (III) 39, 105

Roger (IV) 73

Murchison, Sir Roderick 137

Myddle, truce of 20

National Trust 160

nature reserves 15, 34, 101, 115

New Radnor 102-111

Castle **109**

Church of St Mary 111

George Cornewall Lewis Memorial **103**

history **103**

Oak Inn 110

old houses **110**

and Parliament 103

Newtown School of carvers 41

Nicholson, Thomas 119

Norton 80-89

Castle 58, **80**, 87

Church of St Andrew **89**

history **80**

Impton **86**

Manor 60, **87**

Offa, King 85

Offa's Dyke 61-62, 80-89, **85**

Centre 56, 63

Path 56, 61, 83

orchids 150

Osbern fitz Richard 101

Owain Glyndwr 13, 21, 26, 43, 51, 60, 65, 69, 71, 98, 109, 159

Owain ap Madog 80

Owain ap Maredudd, Sir 141

paganism 2, 119

Pain fitz John 159

Painscastle 158-168

history **159**

Roast Ox **168**

Roundabout **160**

Pales, The 122-129, **123**

Pant Glas **116**

Parker, John 111

Parliament 13, 22, 51, 83, 103

Pearson, J.L. 59, 91

Philips, Francis 22

George 22

Pilleth 68-73

battle of 65, **71**

Church of Our Lady of Pilleth **69**

Court **70**

pillow mounds 117

Port, Roger 101

Porth, Einion o'r 111

Pountney-Smith, S. 59

prehistory **104**; *see also* tumuli

Presteigne 86, 90-101

assizes 99

Broad Street houses **97**, 98

Presteigne (cont.)
  Bryan's Ground **96**
  Castle 101
  Church of St Andrew
    91
  Duke's Arms 99
  history **98**
  Judge's Lodgings **99**
  Radnorshire Arms
    99
  Shire Hall 99
  Warden, the 101
  Withybeds Nature
    Reserve 101
Price, Revd John 163
  Stephen 70

Quakers 123

Radnorshire
  abolition 98
  county court 26
  county town 98
  MPs 13, 22, 51, 83,
    92
  Wildlife Trust 15, 34
railways 9, 56, 83
  Knucklas Viaduct
    49, 50
  Mid Wales Railway
    34, **36**
Rebecca Riots 155

Rhayader 25-30
  Castle **27**
  Church of St
    Clement **25**
  history **26**
  Lost Arc 28
  Old Swan 26
  Royal Oak 26
Rhulen 150-157
  Church of St David
    151
  settlement 151
Rhys ap Dafydd 86
Rhys ap Gruffudd of
  Deheubarth 27, 109,
    140, 159
Rhys ap Tewdur of
  Deheubarth 184
Richard II, King 71
rivers
  Edw 139, 140, 153,
    154, 172, 173
  Ithon 17-18
  Lugg 93
  Marteg 34
  Teme 54, 56
  Wye 26, 27, 28, 34,
    175, 184
Robert ap Gwilym 184
Robertson, Henry 49
Romans 3, 5, 7-8, 33,
    141, 159

St Harmon 31-36
  church 32
  history **32**
  monastery 32
sanctuary 151
Saxons 47, 59, 105,
    119
Scott, Sir George
    Gilbert 89
  Sir Walter 159
Second World War 87,
    98, 160, 181
sheila-na-gig 2
Silver John **114**, 119
Sineford, Robert 57
Sirevan, Davies 55
Speed, John 109
squatters' rights **40**,
    155
SSSI 115
standing stones 104,
    114, 115
Stanlow Tump 106
Stapleton Castle **95**,
    101
stone circles 147
Strata Florida Abbey
    27
Strata Marcella 142

Tamworth, John 87
Taylor, Richard 1

Tecla, Saint 131
  disease 137
Thomas, R.S. 193
Tinboeth Castle, *see*
    Castell Tinboeth
Tomen Castle **120**
Tony family 172
  Ralph 140, 159
  Roger 159
tumuli 32, 47, **104**,
    106, 114, **115**, 124,
    128, **139**, **146**, 147,
    148, 181
Twm Tobacco's Grave
    155
Twyn y Garth **181**

Union, Acts of
  (England and Wales)
    13, 24, 98, 103

Vaughan, Nessa
    Williams 181
Vortigern 32

Walton basin **104**, 105
Warner, Anne 123
  Yardley 123
Warwick, Earls of 159,
    172
Watkins, Alfred 104
Waun Marteg 32

Welsh
  mythology 51
  princes 27, 71, 120,
    170
  raiding parties 86,
    91
  uprisings and mili-
    tary action 27, 58,
    60, 67, 69, 71, 109,
    140, 141
Whimble, the 106
Wilkins, Walter 92
Williams, Jonathan
    139
  S.W. 25
Wilson, Thomas 22
Winton, de, family 160
witchcraft 78
wolves 149
Worthington, W.J. 190
Wye Valley Walk 29,
    34, 189
Wyvern 41

IT'S THE WORLD'S BIRTHDAY TOD